Percy Bysshe Shelley

The wandering Jew

A poem

Percy Bysshe Shelley

The wandering Jew
A poem

ISBN/EAN: 9783337197063

Printed in Europe, USA, Canada, Australia, Japan

Cover: Foto ©Lupo / pixelio.de

More available books at **www.hansebooks.com**

THE WANDERING JEW.

A Poem

BY

PERCY BYSSHE SHELLEY.

Edited

BY BERTRAM DOBELL.

"*If I will that he tarry till I come, what is that to thee? Follow thou me.*"—St. John xxi. 22.

London:
PUBLISHED FOR THE SHELLEY SOCIETY,
BY REEVES AND TURNER, 196, STRAND.
1887.

NOTE.

[THE text of *The Wandering Jew* follows the version printed in *Fraser's Magazine*. But (as I have explained in the Introduction) in the various extracts printed in the *Edinburgh Literary Journal* there are many lines which do not appear in *Fraser's Magazine*. These lines I have inserted in the text, and, in order to distinguish them, and to avoid the necessity of numerous footnotes, they are printed in italics. Readers will therefore please note that all passages in italics appeared in the *Literary Journal* only. Moreover, the selections printed in the *Journal* differ in many minute points of punctuation, spelling, &c., from the *Fraser* version. These variations are noted at the bottom of the page; and readers will understand that the various readings there given (excepting in a few duly specified cases) are from the *Literary Journal*.]

CONTENTS.

	PAGE
INTRODUCTION	xiii
THE WANDERING JEW—	
CANTO I.	1
CANTO II.	17
CANTO III.	27
CANTO IV.	47
APPENDIX—	
THE WANDERING JEW'S SOLILOQUY	69
INTRODUCTORY ARTICLE IN *Fraser's Magazine* . .	71
NOTES	95

INTRODUCTION

INTRODUCTION.

OF all the legends which have obtained popular currency, not one is more remarkable for singularity and suggestiveness than the wild story of the Wandering Jew. However it may have originated, it has had an influence greater probably than any other myth (with the possible exception of the Faust legend) not only upon the minds of unlettered persons, but upon the imaginations of poets, artists, and romance-writers. But, of all the authors who have dealt with the subject, no other seems to have been so strongly influenced by it as was Percy Bysshe Shelley. The Wandering Jew was the subject of his earliest poem of any length; in *Queen Mab* he is one of the most important figures; there are allusions to him in other poems; and in *Hellas*—the last work published during Shelley's lifetime—he makes a most impressive re-appearance. An attempt, therefore, to trace the history of *The Wandering Jew*, and to show (what hitherto has been doubted) that the poem so-named was entirely, or at least almost wholly, Shelley's, can hardly be altogether devoid of interest or importance.

The Wandering Jew has hitherto been omitted from almost all editions of Shelley's works, because the editors, relying upon Medwin's statements, have believed that Shelley's part in it was very small, and that Medwin was really its author, or at least the author of the chief part of it. Medwin indeed asserts as much; and were he a writer of ordinary credit, it would scarcely be possible to dispute his statement. It is certain, however, that, owing to some mental defect, he was a most inaccurate and misleading writer. His statements can hardly ever be depended upon, except when confirmed by independent testimony. I think I can show clearly enough that what he says regarding *The Wandering Jew* is not only inconsistent with itself, but opposed to what we learn from other sources; and, therefore, that we may disregard his assertions altogether, and decide the question of the authorship of the poem independently of his evidence.

The Wandering Jew appears to have been written in 1810, when Shelley was about eighteen years of age. When finished, it was submitted to Messrs. Ballantyne and Co., the Edinburgh publishers, by whom it was declined. Shelley then offered it to Stockdale, at that time a well-known and rather prosperous London publisher. The latter states, however, that it never reached him; a statement about which I have my doubts. In 1827, when

INTRODUCTION.

Stockdale was publishing his scandalous *Budget*, he printed, among other letters of Shelley's, one relating wholly to *The Wandering Jew* and three containing references to it. This letter and these references, before proceeding further, it will be well to reproduce. The letter is written from "Field Place, September 28th, 1810," and is as follows:—

"SIR,—I sent, before I had the pleasure of knowing you, the MS. of a poem to Messrs. Ballantyne and Co., Edinburgh; they have declined publishing it, with the enclosed letter. I now offer it to you, and depend upon your honour as a gentleman for a fair price for the copyright. It will be sent to you from Edinburgh. The subject is *The Wandering Jew*. As to its containing atheistical principles, I assure you I was wholly unaware of the fact hinted at. Your good sense will point out the impossibility of inculcating pernicious doctrines in a poem which, as you will see, is so totally abstract from any circumstances which occur under the possible view of mankind.

"I am, Sir,
"Your obedient and humble servant,
"PERCY B. SHELLEY."

The enclosed letter from Messrs. Ballantyne and Co., declining to publish the poem, is remarkable enough to deserve re-production:—

"Edinburgh, Sept. 24th, 1810.

"SIR,—The delay which occurred in our reply to you, respecting the poem you have obligingly offered us for publication, has arisen from our literary friends and advisers (at least such as we have confidence in) being in the country at this season, as is usual, and the time they have bestowed on its perusal.

"We are extremely sorry at length, after the most mature deliberation, to be under the necessity of declining the honour of being the publishers of the present poem; not that we doubt its success, but that it is perhaps better suited to the character and liberal feelings of the English, than the bigoted spirit which yet pervades many cultivated minds in this country. Even Walter Scott is assailed on all hands, at present, by our Scotch spiritual and evangelical magazines and instructors, for having promulgated atheistical doctrines in *The Lady of the Lake*.

"We beg you will have the goodness to advise us how it should be returned, and we think its being consigned to some person in London would be more likely to ensure its safety than addressing it to Horsham.

"We are, Sir,

"Your most obedient humble servants,

"JOHN BALLANTYNE & CO."

Writing to Stockdale on November 14, 1810, Shelley says:—"I am surprised that you have not received *The Wandering Jew*, and in consequence write to Mr. Ballantyne to mention it; you will, doubtlessly, therefore receive it soon." Writing again to Stockdale on November 19, 1810, he says:—"If you have not got *The Wandering Jew* from Mr. B., I will send you a MS. copy which I possess."

It is to be presumed that Stockdale, in reply, stated that he had not received the copy from Messrs. Ballantyne; and that Shelley thereupon sent him the MS. copy of which he speaks; for in a letter, dated December 2, 1810, he says:—"Will you, if you have got two copies of *The Wandering Jew*, send one of them to me, as I have thought of some corrections which I wish to make; your opinion on it will likewise much oblige me." No further references to *The Wandering Jew* occur in the other letters to Stockdale, nor, so far as I am aware, in any other part of Shelley's correspondence. Doubtless, he soon came to see that it was an immature and comparatively worthless production, and he would have been well content with its entire suppression. It is highly probable that, if he could have reclaimed the two manuscript copies, they would have been committed to the flames. But as both were out of his reach—one reposing quietly at Edinburgh (Shelley's application to Ballantyne and Co. for its return having perhaps miscarried), the other, it may be, lying *perdu* among Stockdale's papers—he probably regarded them as mere "alms for oblivion," and did not contemplate the possibility of their being disinterred and published after his death. But the poem, which its author regarded as dead and buried, underwent a resurrection in 1831, when it was published in the pages of *Fraser's Magazine*. It has hitherto been generally supposed that this was the first appearance of the poem, or of any portion of it, in print. I have ascertained, however, that two years previously, a long article about it, which gave copious extracts from the poem, appeared in *The Edinburgh Literary Journal*. This article adds considerably to our knowledge respecting the poem, and helps to decide the question of its authorship. It was unknown to Medwin, and seems to have remained unknown also to all Shelley's editors and biographers down to the present time. I will now proceed to summarize the chief points of interest in it.

In No. 32 of *The Edinburgh Literary Journal* the following notice appeared :—

"THE POET SHELLEY.

"There has recently been put into our hands a manuscript volume, which we look upon as one of the most remarkable literary curiosities extant. *It is a poem in four cantos, by the late poet Shelley, and entirely written in his own hand.*[1] It is entitled *The Wandering Jew*, and contains many passages of great power and beauty. It was composed upwards of twenty years ago, and brought by the poet to Edinburgh, which he visited about that period. It has since lain in the custody of a literary gentleman of this town, to whom it was then offered for publication. We have received permission to give our readers a further account of its contents, with some extracts, next Saturday; and it affords us much pleasure to have it in our power to be thus instrumental in rescuing, through the medium of the *Literary Journal,* from the obscurity to which it might

---

[1] I have italicized this sentence, because I think it has an important bearing upon the question as to the authorship of the poem.

otherwise have been consigned, one of the earliest and most striking of this gifted poet's productions, the very existence of which has never hitherto been surmised."

Accordingly, in Nos. 33 and 34 (the numbers for June 27 and July 4, 1829) of the *Literary Journal*, the promised account of the poem duly appeared. After giving some particulars, not altogether accurate, as to the time when the poem was written, the article proceeds:—

"It may possibly have been offered to one or two booksellers, both in London and Edinburgh, without success, and this may account for the neglect into which the author allowed it to fall, when new cares crowded upon him, and new prospects opened round him. Certain it is, that it has been carefully kept by the literary gentleman to whom he entrusted its perusal when he visited Edinburgh in 1811, and would have been willingly surrendered by him at any subsequent period, had any application to that effect been made."

The statement that Shelley gave the poem to the "literary gentleman" in 1811, is difficult to reconcile with the fact that it was in 1810 that the poem was submitted to Messrs. Ballantyne and Co. It seems most probable that the copy used by the writer in the *Literary Journal* was the one sent to Ballantyne and Co. in 1810, and that, in the lapse of time, the circumstances under which it had first come into his possession had become somewhat confused in the mind of the "literary gentleman." However, it may have been otherwise, for Shelley certainly visited Edinburgh in 1811 (on the occasion of his marriage with Harriett Westbrook), and he may then have made the acquaintance of the "literary gentleman," and left *The Wandering Jew* in his care. Possibly, being in Edinburgh in 1811, Shelley took the opportunity of reclaiming his poem from Ballantyne and Co., and having then made the acquaintance of the "literary gentleman," may have transferred it to him.

Returning to the article in the *Literary Journal*, the passage following the one already quoted is so interesting, and will be so new to readers of the present day, that I give it in full :—

" Mr. Shelley appears to have had some doubts whether to call his poem *The Wandering Jew* or *The Victim of the Eternal Avenger*. Both names occur in the manuscript; but had the work been published, it is to be hoped that he would finally have fixed on the former, the more especially as the poem itself contains very little calculated to give offence to the religious reader. The motto on the title-page is from the 22nd chapter of St. John :—'If I will that he tarry till I come, what is that to thee ?—follow thou me.' Turning over the leaf, we meet with the following Dedication :—' To Sir Francis Burdett, bart., M.P., in consideration of the active virtues by which both his public and private life is so eminently distinguished, the following poem is inscribed by the Author.' Again turning the leaf, we meet with the—

INTRODUCTION.

"'PREFACE.

"'The subject of the following Poem is an imaginary personage, noted for the various and contradictory traditions which have prevailed concerning him—The Wandering Jew. Many sage monkish writers have supported the authenticity of this fact, the reality of his existence. But as the quoting them would have led me to annotations perfectly uninteresting, although very fashionable, I decline presenting anything to the public but the bare poem, which they will agree with me not to be of sufficient consequence to authorise deep antiquarian researches on its subject. I might, indeed, have introduced, by anticipating future events, the no less grand, although equally groundless, superstitions of the battle of Armageddon, the personal reign of J—— C——, &c.; but I preferred, improbable as the following tale may appear, retaining the old method of describing past events: it is certainly more consistent with reason, more interesting, even in works of imagination. With respect to the omission of elucidatory notes, I have followed the well-known maxim of 'Do unto others as thou wouldest they should do unto thee.'

"'January, 1811.'"

"'The poem introduced by the above Preface is in four cantos; and though the octosyllabic verse is the most prominent, it contains a variety of measures, like Sir Walter Scott's poetical romances. The incidents are simple, and refer rather to an episode in the life of the Wandering Jew, than to any attempt at a full delineation of all his adventures. We shall give an analysis of the plot, and intersperse, as we proceed, some of the most interesting passages of the poem."

Neither the Dedication nor the Preface of the poem, as given above, appeared in *Fraser's Magazine* when the poem was printed in that periodical. Sir Francis Burdett, although he played a prominent part in the political history of the early part of the century, is now so nearly forgotten, that it may be necessary to remind readers of the present day that he was one of the most advanced radicals of that time; and hence it was very natural that Shelley should dedicate his poem to him. The passage accounting for the absence of annotations is a side-blow at Sir Walter Scott, and rather an unfair one, considering that *The Wandering Jew* bears evident tokens that its author had diligently studied Scott's poetical romances. It is likely enough that the hit at the superstitions of the battle of Armageddon, the personal reign of J—— C——,[1] &c., rather than anything in the poem itself, was the chief cause of its rejection by Ballantyne and Co. No more than this one passage would have been needed to convict the author of *The Wandering Jew* of blasphemy in the eyes of those preternaturally acute fanatics who could discover atheism in *The Lady of the Lake*. But, in truth, a careful reading of Shelley's poem shows that it contains

[1] It is, of course, very unlikely that Shelley adopted the device of giving the initials only of the name of Christ, and it was doubtless printed thus by the editor of the *Literary Journal* out of a fear of offending his more scrupulous readers.

several passages which it would be hard to reconcile with orthodox opinions, and which may well have made Messrs. Ballantyne and Co. pause before undertaking the responsibility of publishing it. It is rather curious that the preface should be dated "January, 1811," considering that the MS. was placed in the hands of Messrs. Ballantyne at least three months before that time; but perhaps Shelley reckoned that it could not be published during 1810, and for that reason chose to date it in advance.

There is not much else in the article on *The Wandering Jew* which need be quoted, the chief part of it being devoted to a summary of the incidents of the poem, accompanied with various illustrative extracts from it. I must not, however, omit the following:—

"It is curious to observe, before proceeding to the second canto, that, in illustration of something said by Paulo, Shelley quotes, in the margin, the following line from Æschylus, so remarkably applicable to his own future fate,—

$$\text{'Εμȣ θανόντος γαια μιχθητο πο ζι.'}$$ "

The writer of the article by no means agrees with its later critics as to the worthlessness of the poem; on the contrary he expresses great admiration for certain parts of the work. The extracts given from it differ materially from the corresponding passages as printed in *Fraser's Magazine*, and prove, with sufficient certainty, that the manuscript used by the writer in the *Literary Journal* could not have been the same as the one used by *Fraser*.

Reviewing the evidence as to the authorship of the poem, which may be derived from the various sources I have mentioned, we see that Shelley uniformly appears as the sole author, and that there is nowhere a hint as to his having had a coadjutor in the work. The manuscript is written entirely in Shelley's own handwriting; he dedicates it to Sir Francis Burdett; the Preface contains no hint that he had received assistance in writing it; and he offers it as his own production to Ballantyne and Co. and to Stockdale. It is noteworthy that in writing to Stockdale about it, he says:—"I now offer it to you, and depend upon your honour as a gentleman for a fair price for the copyright." There could hardly be a more absolute assertion of his authorship of the poem than this, for it can hardly be supposed that Shelley would ask for money for the copyright of a poem which was not his to dispose of.

If we now turn to Medwin's statements with regard to *The Wandering Jew*, and examine them carefully, we shall, I think, find them to be so loose and contradictory as to be altogether unworthy of credit. Medwin first referred to the poem in 1833 in *The Shelley Papers*.[1] After speaking of a ballad which, he says, was Shelley's first production, and which was written when he was about fifteen, he proceeds:—

"Shortly afterwards we wrote, in conjunction, six or seven cantos on the subject of the Wandering Jew, of

---

[1] The book with this title was first published in 1833, but the chief part of its contents had previously appeared in the *Athenæum* during 1832.

which the first four, with the exception of a very few lines, were exclusively mine. It was a thing such as boys usually write, a *cento* from different favourite authors; the crucifixion scene altogether a plagiary from a volume of Cambridge Prize Poems. The part which I contributed I have still, and was surprised to find *totidem verbis* in *Fraser's Magazine*. . . . As might be shown by the last cantos of that poem, which *Fraser* did not think worth publishing,[1] his [Shelley's] ideas were, at that time, strange and incomprehensible, mere elements of thought—images wild, vast and Titanic."

It will be observed that Medwin here claims the first *four* cantos as being exclusively his own, "with the exception of a very few lines." He also speaks of the last cantos of that poem, "which *Fraser* did not think worth publishing." Now the fact is, that both in the *Edinburgh Literary Journal* and in *Fraser* the poem is stated to be *complete*. The former says:—"The poem introduced by the above Preface is in four cantos;" while *Fraser*, in the prefatory remarks on the poem, testifies to the same effect:—"The important literary curiosity which the liberality of the gentleman into whose hands it has fallen, enables us now to lay before the public for the first time, *in a complete state,* was offered for publication by Mr. Shelley when quite a boy." It thus

---

[1] It is worth noting that Medwin afterwards stated that the portion of the poem written by Shelley was by far the best; yet, if we believe the statement he makes here, it was Shelley's portion which *Fraser*, "did not think worth publishing."

appears that Medwin knew so little about the poem that he imagined it to be in six or seven cantos, whereas it was complete in four. He also says that *Fraser* did not think the last cantos worth publishing, whereas *Fraser* certainly published the four cantos in the belief that they constituted a complete poem. Moreover (as I have already pointed out), we cannot put faith in Medwin's statements unless we are prepared to believe that Shelley offered to sell for publication, as his own production, a poem which was not only not his to dispose of, but which was not even a complete work. It seems to me that it is impossible to believe this; and I, at least, prefer to think that Medwin was under the influence of some strange hallucination with regard to the poem.

In his *Life of Shelley*, published in 1847, Medwin gives another and longer account of *The Wandering Jew*. He there says :—

"Shelley, having abandoned prose for poetry, now formed a *grand* design, a metrical romance on the subject of the Wandering Jew, of which the first three cantos were, with a few additions and alterations, almost entirely mine. It was a sort of thing such as boys usually write, a *cento* from different favourite authors; the vision in the third canto taken from Lewis's *Monk*, of which, in common with Byron, he was a great admirer; and the crucifixion scene altogether a plagiarism from a volume of Cambridge Prize Poems. The part which I supplied is still in my possession. After seven or eight cantos were *perpetrated*, Shelley sent them to Campbell for his opinion on their merits, with a view to publication. The author of the *Pleasures of Hope* returned the MS. with the remark that there were only two good lines in it:

> It seemed as if an angel's sigh
> Had breathed the plaintive symphony.

Lines, by the way, savouring strongly of Walter Scott. This criticism of Campbell's gave a death-blow to our hopes of immortality, and so little regard did Shelley entertain for the production, that he left it at his lodgings in Edinburgh, where it was disinterred by some correspondent of Fraser's, and in whose magazine, in 1831, four of the cantos appeared. The others he very wisely did not think worth publishing.

"It must be confessed that Shelley's contributions to this juvenile attempt were far the best, and those, with my MS. before me, I could, were it worth while, point out, though the contrast in the style, and the inconsequence of the opinions on religion, particularly in the last canto, are sufficiently obvious to mark two different hands, and show which passages were his....... The finale of *The Wandering Jew* is also Shelley's, and proves that thus early he had imbibed opinions which were often the subject of our controversies. We differed also as to the conduct of the poem. It was my wish to follow the German fragment, and put an end to the Wandering Jew—a consummation Shelley would by no means consent to."

The above appears to me to be a passage remarkable for confusion of thought and inexactitude of statement. I doubt if even one of the several statements which the paragraph contains, represents quite correctly the facts of the case. The impression it makes upon me is, that Medwin's ideas and recollections about the poem had grown so confused that he was totally unable to give a clear and connected account of the matter. Shelley, we are told, formed a *grand* design, yet, strangely enough, the first three cantos (or, according to *The Shelley Papers*, the first four cantos) of the *grand* design were written by Medwin. We are next informed that:—"It was a sort of thing such as boys usually write,"—but, however juvenile an effort the poem may be, it is certainly not the sort of thing boys usually write. Again, it is said that Lewis's *Monk* is the source of the vision in the third canto. It is true that one of the characters in this romance experiences a vision, but it bears little or no resemblance to the vision in the poem. What Medwin should have said, is, that the whole idea of the poem was probably derived from *The Monk*. In that curious production, which at once delighted and scandalized our grandfathers and grandmothers, the Wandering Jew is an important figure; and several of the circumstances of Shelley's poem are derived from Lewis's romance. "The crucifixion scene, altogether a plagiarism from a volume of Cambridge Prize Poems," is another assertion which is certainly not literally true. The Seatonian poem for 1765, called "The Crucifixion," by Thomas Zouch, is doubtless the one Medwin alludes to. It is written in blank verse, and although it contains passages which bear some resemblance to the crucifixion scene in *The Wandering Jew*, yet these resemblances are not greater than might be expected to occur in two writers who chose the same subject. The images and expressions are, in fact, such as would naturally occur to any one writing upon the crucifixion, and Shelley no more plagiarises from Zouch, than Zouch does from the New Testament. "The part which I supplied is still in my possession"—how strange then that he did not know whether he had written three or four cantos! "After seven or eight cantos were *perpetrated*,"—but, as I have shown, it was complete, at least as far as Shelley was concerned, in *four* cantos. Moreover, Medwin in 1833 says *six or seven* cantos, but in 1845 he says *seven or eight*. It is very noteworthy that Medwin says nothing about the poem having been offered for publication to Ballantyne and Co., and to Stockdale, which he would surely have done had he known the facts. Indeed, he implies his ignorance on this point by saying that Campbell's adverse opinion extinguished Shelley's interest in the poem, which, as we know, it certainly did not.

I could point out other discrepancies in Medwin's statements, but it is surely unnecessary to do so. His whole account of the poem is so vitiated by contradictions and inaccuracies that no part of it can be depended upon. On the other hand, there is nothing that I know of to lead us to doubt that Shelley, in claiming the authorship of the poem, was perfectly justified by the facts of the case. In short, the conclusions I have come to from a consideration of the various circumstances, are, that the original design was Shelley's (this even Medwin allows); that he wrote (possibly with some slight assistance from Medwin) the four cantos as we now have them; that some discussion may have taken place between them with regard to a continuation of the poem, but that Shelley ultimately decided not to extend it. At the same time, it is likely enough that Medwin may have written something of the same sort on his own account, and he may possibly, in the course of time, have confused his own poem with Shelley's, and thus have come to believe himself the author of the latter.

I have already stated that the extracts printed in the *Literary Journal* differ very considerably from the corresponding passages in *Fraser*. In addition to numerous minute variations, the former contains many lines which do not appear in the latter. Thus, if we take the opening section of the poem, we shall find that while *Fraser* gives nineteen lines only, there are twenty-eight lines in the *Literary Journal*. If I might hazard a guess as to the cause of the differences in the two versions, I should say that the one used by the *Literary Journal* was a carefully revised and finished manuscript, while the one used by *Fraser* was probably a rough draft of the poem as originally composed. I also imagine that the former was the copy submitted to Messrs. Ballantyne and Co., while the latter was the one sent by Shelley to Stockdale, which may or may not have reached him, but which, I think, must have remained in the custody of some one in London until the thought occurred to its custodian of offering it for publication to *Fraser's Magazine*. Of course I only put forward these opinions as probable hypotheses, which further evidence may disprove: but they seem to me to be the ones which best fit in with the circumstances of the case, so far as they are at present known.

What has become of these two manuscripts? I can hardly think that both of them have been destroyed; and it is rather curious, considering the avidity with which collectors have sought for Shelley's letters and manuscripts, that neither of them has yet been brought to light. But I do not think we need yet despair of recovering at least one of them.

It may very probably be questioned whether the object I have here had in view—namely, to prove that Shelley was responsible for a poem of very indifferent merit—was one which it was worth while to undertake or accomplish. Since Medwin had claimed it, why not leave him in possession of it? With *Zastrozzi* and *St. Irvyne* to answer for, why add *The Wandering Jew* to the list of Shelley's juvenile failures? To this it might be sufficient to reply, that the search for truth justifies itself, and needs no apology, whatever may result from it. But just as we look with interest and instruction at the first rough sketches which have formed the foundation for some grand design, so, if we look upon the early works of Shelley as preparatory studies for his mature masterpieces, they will be seen to possess an importance which their merits certainly do not give them. An author's failures are no less instructive than his successes; and, perhaps, from a psychological standpoint, *The Wandering Jew* deserves attentive study, although the student certainly will not and need not linger over it as he will over *Prometheus Unbound*. *The Two Gentlemen of Verona* and *Love's Labour's Lost* might be well spared from the list of Shakespeare's productions, if their merits only were considered; but they help us, in a way which his greater works do not, to understand the growth and development of his genius. Had Shelley's critical faculty developed itself as early as his faculty of expression, we should certainly not have had his two novels, or *The Wandering Jew*; but possibly we might not have had *Prometheus* either. A poet learns far more by attempting to create a poem or a play, than by reflecting, for however long a time, upon the right method of creating them. As the art of swimming cannot possibly be learned without going into the water, so it is impossible to learn how to write poetry, without attempting to compose it; and this naturally involves the production of much indifferent verse. Of course the real poet soon comes to perceive the worthlessness of his early writings, but it is a misfortune if he perceives their small value at the very time he composes them; for when this is the case his invention is chilled and discouraged, and he is apt to abandon his efforts in despair. The critical faculty, in short, when in excess, is a hindrance, rather than a help, and we have reason to rejoice that, in Shelley's case, it was not developed too early. If we cannot allow any positive good qualities to *The Wandering Jew* (and truth compels me to say that I cannot perceive any merits in it beyond a certain facility of versification and some few powerful lines), we need not regret that it was written, for doubtless its composition rendered easier the task of creating the great works which have placed Shelley among the Immortals.

BERTRAM DOBELL.

THE WANDERING JEW.

THE WANDERING JEW.

CANTO I.

"Me miserable, which way shall I fly?
Infinite wrath and infinite despair—
Which way I fly is hell—myself am hell;
And in this lowest deep a lower deep,
To which the hell I suffer seems a heaven."
Paradise Lost.

THE brilliant orb of parting day
Diffused a rich and mellow ray,[1]
Above the mountain's brow;
It tinged the hills with lustrous light,
It tinged the promontory's height,
Still sparkling with the snow;
And[2] as aslant it threw its beam,
Tipt[3] with gold the mountain stream

---

[1] and a mellow ray [2] And, [3] Tipp'd

THE WANDERING JEW.

That laved the vale below;¹
Long hung the eye of glory there, 10
And linger'd as if loth to leave
A scene so lovely and so fair.
'Twere luxury even, there to grieve.²
So soft the clime, so balm the air,
So pure and genial were the skies, 15
In sooth 'twas almost Paradise,—
For ne'er did the sun's splendour close
On such a picture of repose ;—
All, all was tranquil, all was still,
Save when³ the music of the rill, 20
Or⁴ distant waterfall,
At intervals broke on the ear,
Which echo's⁵ self was charmed⁶ to hear,
And ceased her babbling call.
With every charm the landscape glow'd 25
Which partial Nature's hand bestow'd;
Nor could the mimic hand of art
Such beauties or such hues impart.

Light clouds⁷ in fleeting livery gay,
Hung,⁸ painted in grotesque array 30

¹ below.   ² 'Twere there even luxury to grieve;
   ³ where—probably a printer's error.
   ⁴ Or a   ⁵ Echo's   ⁶ pleased
         ⁷ clouds,   ⁸ Hung

Upon the western sky:
Forgetful of the approaching dawn,
The peasants danced upon the lawn,
For the vintage time was nigh:
How jocund to the tabor's sound, 35
O'er the smooth, trembling turf they bound,[1]
In every measure light and free,
The very soul of harmony;[2]
Grace in each attitude, they move,
They thrill to amorous ecstasy, 40
Light as the dewdrops of the morn,
That hang upon the blossomed[3] thorn,
Subdued by the pow'r of resistless Love.
Ah! days of innocence, of joy,
Of rapture that knows no alloy, 45
Haste on,—ye roseate hours,
Free from the world's tumultuous cares,
From pale distrust, from hopes and fears,
Baneful concomitants of time,—
'Tis yours, beneath this favour'd clime, 50
Your pathway strewn with flowers,
Upborne on pleasure's downy wing,
To quaff a long unfading spring,
And beat with light and careless step the ground;

---

[1] The smooth turf trembling as they bound,
[2] !   [3] blossom'd

The fairest flowers too soon grow sere, 55
Too soon shall tempests blast the year,
And sin's eternal winter reign around.

But see, what forms are those,
Scarce seen by glimpse of dim twilight,
Wandering o'er the mountain's height? 60
They swiftly haste to the vale below:
One wraps his mantle around his brow,
As if to hide his woes;
And as his steed impetuous flies,
What strange fire flashes from his eyes! 65
The far off city's murmuring sound
Was borne on the breeze which floated around;
Noble Padua's lofty spire
Scarce glow'd with the sunbeam's latest fire,
Yet dashed the travellers on— 70
Ere night o'er the earth was spread,
Full many a mile they must have sped,
Ere their destined course was run.
Welcome was the moonbeam's ray,
Which slept upon the towers so grey. 75
But, hark! a convent's vesper bell—
It seemed to be a very spell—
The stranger checked his courser's rein,
And listened to the mournful sound:
Listened—and paused—and paused again: 80

A thrill of pity and of pain
Through his inmost soul had past,
While gushed the tear-drops silently and fast.

A crowd was at the convent gate,
The gate was opened wide;   85
No longer on his steed he sate,
But mingled with the tide.
He felt a solemn awe and dread,
As he the chapel entered;
Dim was the light from the pale moon beaming,   90
As it fell on the saint-cyphered[1] panes;[2]
Or from the western window streaming,
Tinged the pillars with varied stains.
To the eye of enthusiasm strange forms were gliding[3]
In each dusky recess of the aisle;   95
And indefined shades in succession were striding,
O'er the coignes[4] of the gothic pile.[5]
The pillars to the vaulted roof
In airy lightness rose ;
Now they mount to the rich Gothic ceiling aloof,   100
And exquisite tracery disclose.

The altar illumined now darts its bright rays,

---

[1] saint-cipher'd   [2] ,   [3] gliding,
[4] Buttress nor coigne of vantage.—*Macbeth.* (Author's Note.)
[5] pillar'd pile;—

THE WANDERING JEW.

The train past in brilliant array;
On the shrine Saint Pietro's rich ornaments blaze,
And rival the brilliance of day   105
Hark!—now the loud organ swells full on the ear—
So sweetly mellow, chaste, and clear;
Melting, kindling, raising, firing,
Delighting now, and now inspiring,
Peal upon peal the music floats—   110
Now they list still as death to the dying notes;
Whilst the soft voices of the choir,
Exalt the soul from base desire;
Till it mounts on unearthly pinions free,
Dissolved in heavenly ecstasy.   115

Now a dead stillness reigned around,
Uninterrupted by a sound;
Save when in deadened response ran,
The last faint echoes down the aisle,
Reverberated through the pile,   120
As within the pale the holy man,
With voice devout and saintly look,
Slow chaunted from the sacred book,
Or pious prayers were duly said,
For spirits of departed dead.   125
With beads and crucifix and hood,
Close by his side the abbess stood;
Now her dark penetrating eyes

Were raised in suppliance to heaven,
And now her bosom heaved with sighs,   130
As if to human weakness given.
Her stern, severe, yet beauteous brow
Frowned on all who stood below;
And the fire which flashed from her steady gaze,
As it turned on the listening crowd its rays,   135
Superior virtue told,—
Virtue as pure as heaven's own dew,
But which, untainted, never knew,
To pardon weaker mould.
The heart though chaste and cold as snow—   140
'Twere faulty to be virtuous so.

Not a whisper now breathed in the pillared aisle—
The stranger advanced to the altar high—
Convulsive was heard a smothered sigh!
Lo! four fair nuns to the altar draw near,   145
With solemn footstep, as the while
A fainting novice they bear—
The roses from her cheek are fled
But there the lily reigns instead;
Light as a sylph's, her form confest,   150
Beneath the drapery of her vest,
A perfect grace and symmetry;
Her eyes, with rapture form'd to move,
To melt with tenderness and love,

Or beam with sensibility, 155
To Heaven were raised in pious prayer,
A silent eloquence of woe;
Now hung the pearly tear-drop there,
Sate on her cheek a fix'd despair;
And now she beat her bosom bare, 160
As pure as driven snow.
Nine graceful novices [1] around
Fresh roses strew [2] upon the ground:
In purest white arrayed, [3]
Nine [4] spotless vestal virgins shed 165
Sabæan [5] incense o'er the head
Of the devoted maid.

They dragged her to the altar's pale,
The traveller leant against the rail,
And gazed with eager eye,— 170
His cheek was flushed with sudden glow,
On his brow sate a darker shade of woe,
As a transient expression fled by.

The sympathetic feeling flew
Thro' every breast, from man to man, 175
Confused and open clamours ran,
Louder and louder still they grew;

[1] Novices   [2] strew'd   [3] array'd;   [4] Three   [5] Sabean

When the abbess waved her hand,
A stern resolve was in her eye,
And every wild tumultuous cry   180
Was stilled at her command.

The abbess made the well known sign—
The novice reached the fatal shrine,
And mercy implored from the power divine;
At length she shrieked aloud,   185
She dashed from the supporting nun,
Ere the fatal rite was done,
And plunged amid the crowd.
Confusion reigned throughout the throng,
Still the novice fled along,   190
Impelled by frantic fear,
When the maddened traveller's eager grasp
In firmest yet in wildest clasp
Arrested her career.
As fainting from terror she sank on the ground,   195
Her loosened locks floated her fine form around;
The zone which confined her shadowy vest
No longer her throbbing bosom prest,
Its animation dead;
No more her feverish pulse beat high,   200
Expression dwelt not in her eye,
Her wildered senses fled.

    *   *   *   *   *

Hark! Hark! the demon of the storm!
I see his vast expanding form
Blend with the strange and sulphurous glare 205
Of comets through the turbid air.
Yes, 'twas his voice, I heard its roar,
The wild waves lashed the caverned shore
In angry murmurs hoarse and loud,
Higher and higher still they rise; 210
Red lightnings gleam from every cloud
And paint wild shapes upon the skies;
The echoing thunder rolls around,
Convulsed with earthquake rocks the ground.

The traveller yet undaunted stood, 215
He heeded not the roaring flood;
Yet Rosa slept, her bosom bare,
Her cheek was deadly pale,
The ringlets of her auburn hair
Streamed in a lengthened trail, 220
And motionless her seraph form;
Unheard, unheeded raved the storm.
Whilst, borne on the wing of the gale,
The harrowing shriek of the white sea-mew
As o'er the midnight surge she flew; 225
The howlings of the squally blast
As o'er the beetling cliffs it past;
Mingled with the peals on high,

That, swelling louder, echoed by,
Assailed the traveller's ear.   230
He heeded not the maddened storm
As it pelted against his lofty form,
He felt no awe, no fear.
In contrast, like the courser pale [1]
That stalks along Death's pitchy vale   235
With silent, with gigantic tread,
Trampling the dying and the dead.

Rising from her death-like trance,
Fair Rosa met the stranger's glance;
She started from his chilling gaze,   240
Wild was it as the tempest's blaze,
It shot a lurid gleam of light.
A secret spell of sudden dread,
A mystic, strange, and harrowing fear,
As when the spirits of the dead,   245
Drest in ideal shapes appear,
And hideous glance on human sight—
Scarce could Rosa's frame sustain,
The chill that pressed upon her brain.

Anon, that transient spell was o'er,   250
Dark clouds deform his brow no more,

[1] "Behold a pale horse, and his name that sate upon him was Death, and Hell followed with him."—*Revelations*, vi. 8. (Author's Note.)

But rapid fled away;
Sweet fascination dwelt around,
Mixed with a soft, a silver sound,
As soothing to the ravished ear, 255
As what enthusiast lovers hear;
Which seems to steal along the sky,
When mountain mists are seen to fly,
Before the approach of day.
He seized on wondering Rosa's hand, 260
"And, ah!" cried he, "be this the band
Shall join us, till this earthly frame,
Sinks convulsed in bickering flame—
When around the demons yell,
And drag the sinful wretch to hell, 265
Then, Rosa, will we part—
Then fate, and only fate's decree,
Shall tear thy lovely soul from me,
And rend thee from my heart.
Long has Paulo sought in vain, 270
A friend to share his grief,—
Never will he seek again,
For the wretch has found relief,
Till the Prince of Darkness bursts his chain,
Till death and desolation reign— 275
Rosa, wilt thou then be mine?
Ever fairest, I am thine!"

He ceased, and on the howling blast,
Which wildly round the mountain past,
Died his accents low ;   280
Yet fiercely howled the midnight storm,
As Paulo bent his awful form,
And leaned his lofty brow.

Rosa.

" Stranger, mystic stranger, rise ;
Whence do these tumults fill the skies ?   285
Who conveyed me, say, this night,
To this wild and cloud-capped height ?
Who art thou ? and why am I
Beneath Heaven's pityless canopy ?
For the wild winds roar around my head ;   290
Lightnings redden the wave ;—
Was it the power of the mighty dead,
Who live beneath the grave ?
Or did the Abbess drag me here,
To make yon swelling surge my bier ? "   295

Paulo.

" Ah, lovely Rosa ! cease thy fear,
It was thy friend who bore thee here—
I, thy friend, till this fabric of earth,
Sinks in the chaos that gave it birth ;
Till the meteor-bolt of the God above,   300

Shall tear its victim from his love,—
That love which must unbroken last,
Till the hour of envious fate is past;
Till the mighty basements of the sky
In bickering hell-flames heated fly: 305
E'en then will I sit on some rocky height,
Whilst around lower clouds of eternal night,
E'en then will I loved Rosa save
From the yawning abyss of the grave.—
Or, into the gulf impetuous hurled— 310
If sinks with its latest tenants the world,
Then will our souls in union fly
Throughout the wide and boundless sky:
Then, free from th' ills that envious fate
Has heaped upon our mortal state, 315
We'll taste etherial pleasure;
Such as none but thou canst give,—
Such as none but I receive,
And rapture without measure."

As thus he spoke, a sudden blaze 320
Of pleasure mingled in his gaze:
Illumined by the dazzling light,
He glows with radiant lustre bright;
His features with new glory shine,
And sparkle as with beams divine. 325
"Strange, awful being," Rosa said,

"Whence is this superhuman dread,
That harrows up my inmost frame?
Whence does this unknown tingling flame,
Consume and penetrate my soul? 330
By turns with fear and love possessed,
Tumultuous thoughts swell high my breast;
A thousand wild emotions roll,
And mingle their resistless tide;
O'er thee some magic arts preside; 335
As by the influence of a charm.
Lulled into rest my griefs subside,
And safe in thy protecting arm,
I feel no power can do me harm:
But the storm raves wildly o'er the sea, 340
Bear me away! I confide in thee!"

CANTO II.

> " I could a tale unfold, whose slightest word
> Would harrow up thy soul, freeze thy young blood,
> Make thy two eyes, like stars, start from their spheres;
> Thy knotted and combined locks to part,
> And each particular hair to stand on end,
> Like quills upon the fretful porcupine."—*Hamlet.*

THE horrors of the mighty blast,
The lowering tempest clouds were past,
Had sunk beneath the main;
Light baseless mists were all that fled, 345
Above the weary traveller's head,
As he left the spacious plain.

Fled were the vapours of the night,
Faint streaks of rosy tinted light
Were painted on the matin grey; 350
And as the sun began to rise,
To pour his animating ray,
Glowed with his fire the eastern skies,
The distant rocks—the far-off bay,

The ocean's sweet and lovely blue, 355
The mountain's variegated breast,
Blushing with tender tints of dawn,
Or with fantastic shadows drest.
The waving wood, the opening lawn,
Rose to existence, waked anew, 360
In colours exquisite of hue,
Their mingled charms Victorio viewed,
And lost in admiration stood.

From yesternight how changed the scene,
When howled the blast o'er the dark cliffs' side, 365
And mingled with the maddened roar
Of the wild surge that lashed the shore.
To-day—scarce heard the whispering breeze,
And still and motionless the seas
Scarce heard the murmuring of their tide; 370
All, all is peaceful and serene,
Serenely on Victorio's breast
It breathed a soft and tranquil rest,
Which bade each wild emotion cease,
And hushed the passions into peace. 375

Along the winding Po he went,
His footsteps to the spot were bent
Where Paulo dwelt, his wandered friend,
For thither did his wishes tend.

Noble Victorio's race was proud, 380
From Cosmo's blood he came;
To him a wild untutored crowd
Of vassals, in allegiance bowed,
Illustrious was his name;
Yet vassals and wealth he scorned, to go 385
Unnoticed with a man of woe:
Gay hope and expectation sate,
Throned in his eager eye,
And ere he reached the castle gate,
The sun had mounted high. 390

Wild was the spot where the castle stood,
Its towers embosomed deep in wood,
Gigantic cliffs, with craggy steeps,
Reared their proud heads on high,
Their bases were washed by the foaming deeps, 395
Their summits were hid in the sky;
From the valley below they excluded the day,
That valley ne'er cheered by the sunbeam's ray;
Nought broke on the silence drear,
Save the hungry vultures darting by, 400
Or eagles yelling fearfully,
As they bore to the rocks their prey,
Or when the fell wolf ravening prowled,
Or the gaunt wild boar fiercely howled
His hideous screams on the night's dull ear. 405

Borne on pleasure's downy wing,
Downy as the breath of spring,
Not thus fled Paulo's hours away,
Though brightened by the cheerful day:
Friendship or wine, or softer love,   410
The sparkling eye, the foaming bowl,
Could with no lasting rapture move,
Nor still the tumults of his soul.
And yet there was in Rosa's kiss
A momentary thrill of bliss;   415
Oft the dark clouds of grief would fly,
Beneath the beams of sympathy;
And love and converse sweet bestow,
A transient requiem from woe.—

Strange business, and of import vast,   420
On things which long ago were past,
Drew Paulo oft from home;
Then would a darker, deeper shade,
By sorrow traced, his brow o'erspread
And o'er his features roam.   425
Oft as they spent the midnight hour,
And heard the wintry wild winds rave
Midst the roar and spray of the dashing wave,
Was Paulo's dark brow seen to lour.
Then, as the lamp's uncertain blaze   430
Shed o'er the hall its partial rays,

And shadows strange were seen to fall,
And glide upon the dusky wall,
Would Paulo start with sudden fear.
Why then unbidden gush'd the tear, 435
As he mutter'd strange words to the ear ?—
Why frequent heaved the smother'd sigh ?—
Why did he gaze on vacancy,
As if some strange form was near?
Then would the fillet of his brow 440
Fierce as a fiery furnace glow,
As it burn'd with red and lambent flame,
Then would cold shuddering seize his frame,
As gasping he labour'd for breath.
The strange light of his gorgon eye, 445
As,[1] frenzied and rolling dreadfully,
It glared with terrific gleam,
Would chill like the spectre gaze of death,
As,[1] conjured by feverish dream,
He seems o'er the sick man's couch to stand, 450
And shakes the dread lance in his skeleton hand.

But when the paroxysm was o'er,
And clouds deform'd his brow no more,
Would Rosa soothe his tumults dire,
Would bid him calm his grief, 455
Would quench reflection's rising fire,

[1] The comma is omitted in *Fraser*.

And give his soul relief.
As on his form with pitying eye,
The ministering angel hung,
And wiped the drops of agony,   460
The music of her syren[1] tongue
Lull'd forcibly his griefs to rest,[2]
Like fleeting visions of the dead,
Or midnight dreams, his sorrows fled:
Waked to new life through all his soul   465
A soft delicious languor stole,
And lapt in heavenly ecstasy
He sank and fainted on her breast.

'Twas on an eve, the leaf was sere,
Howl'd the blast round the castle drear,   470
The boding night-bird's hideous cry
Was mingled with the warning sky;
Heard was the distant torrent's dash,
Seen was the lightning's dark red flash.
As it gleamed on the stormy cloud;   475
Heard was the troubled ocean's roar,
As its wild waves lash'd the rocky shore;
The thunder mutter'd loud,

---

[1] siren
[2] A full stop instead of a comma is given here in the *Literary Journal.*

As wilder still the lightnings flew;
Wilder as the tempest blew, 480
More wildly strange their converse grew.

They talk'd of the ghosts of the mighty dead,
If, when the spark of life were fled,
They visited this world of woe?
Or, were it but a phantasy, 485
Deceptive to the feverish eye,
When strange forms flashed upon the sight,
And stalk'd along at the dead of night?
Or if, in the realms above,
They still, for mortals left below, 490
Retain'd the same affection's glow,
In friendship or in love?—
Debating thus, a pensive train,
Thought upon thought began to rise;
Her thrilling wild harp Rosa took; 495
What sounds in softest murmurs broke
From the seraphic strings!
Celestials borne on odorous wings,
Caught the dulcet melodies,
The life-blood ebb'd in every vein, 500
As Paulo listen'd to the strain.

SONG.

"What sounds are those that float upon the air,[1]
As if to bid the fading day farewell,—
What form is that so shadowy, yet so fair,
Which glides along the rough and pathless dell? 505

Nightly those sounds swell full upon the breeze,
Which seems to sigh as if in sympathy;
They hang amid yon cliff-embosom'd trees,
Or float in dying cadence through the sky.

Now rests that form upon the moonbeam pale, 510
In piteous strains of woe its vesper sings;
Now—now it traverses the silent vale,
Borne on transparent ether's viewless wings.

Oft will it rest beside yon abbey's[2] tower,
Which lifts its ivy-mantled mass so high; 515
Rears its dark head to meet the storms that lour,
And braves the trackless tempests of the sky.

That form, the embodied spirit of a maid,
Forced by a perjured lover to the grave;
A desperate fate the madden'd girl obey'd, 520
And from the dark cliffs plung'd into the wave.

---

[1] The 'turned commas' at the commencement of this line are omitted both in *Fraser*, and in the *Literary Journal*.

[2] Abbey's

There the deep murmurs of the restless surge,
The mournful shriekings of the white sea-mew,
The warring waves, the wild winds, sang her dirge,
And o'er her bones the dark red coral grew.   525

Yet though that form be sunk beneath the main,
Still rests her spirit where its vows were given;
Still fondly visits each loved spot again,
And pours its sorrows on the ear of Heaven.

That spectre wanders through the abbey[1] dale,   530
And suffers pangs which such a fate must share;
Early her soul sank in death's darken'd vale,
And ere long all of us must meet her there."

She ceased, and on the listening ear
Her pensive accents died;   535
So sad they were, so softly clear,
It seemed as if some angel's sigh
Had breathed the plaintive symphony;
So ravishingly sweet their close,
The tones awakened Paulo's woes;   540
Oppressive recollections rose,
And poured their bitter tide.

---

[1] Abbey

Absorbed awhile in grief he stood;
At length he seemed as one inspired,
His burning fillet blazed with blood— 545
A lambent flame his features fired.
"The hour is come, the fated hour;
Whence is this new, this unfelt power?—
Yes, I've a secret to unfold,
And such a tale as ne'er was told, 550
A dreadful, dreadful mystery!
Scenes, at whose retrospect e'en now,
Cold drops of anguish on my brow,
The icy chill of death I feel:
Wrap, Rosa, bride, thy breast in steel, 555
Thy soul with nerves of iron brace,
As to your eyes I darkly trace,
My sad, my cruel destiny.

"Victorio, lend your ears, arise,
Let us seek the battling skies, 560
Wild o'er our heads the thunder crashing,
And at our feet the wild waves dashing;
As tempest, clouds, and billows roll,
In gloomy concert with my soul.
Rosa, follow me— 565
For my soul is joined to thine,
And thy being's linked to mine—
Rosa, list to me."

CANTO III.

> "His form had not yet lost
> All its original brightness, nor appeared
> Less than archangel ruined, and the excess
> Of glory obscured; but his face
> Deep scars of thunder had intrenched, and care
> Sate on his faded cheek."—*Paradise Lost.*

PAULO.

"'Tis sixteen hundred years ago,
Since I came from Israel's land; 570
Sixteen hundred years of woe!—
With deep and furrowing hand,
God's mark is painted on my head;
Must there remain until the dead
Hear the last trump, and leave the tomb, 575
And earth spouts fire from her riven womb.

"*How can I paint that dreadful day,*
That time of terror and dismay,
When, for our sins, a Saviour died,
And the meek Lamb was crucified! 580

As dread that day, when [1] borne along
To slaughter by the insulting throng,
Infuriate for Deicide,
I mock'd [2] our Saviour, and I cried,
Go, go,[3] 'Ah! I will go,' said he,[4] 585
'Where scenes of endless bliss invite;[5]
To the blest regions of the light [6]
I go, but thou shalt here remain—[7]
Thou diest not till I come again'—[8]
E'en now, by horror traced, I see 590
His perforated feet and hands;
The madden'd crowd around him stands.[9]
Pierces his side the ruffian spear,
Big rolls the bitter anguish'd tear.[10]
Hark, that deep groan!—he dies—he dies.[11] 595
And breathes, in death's last agonies,
Forgiveness to his enemies. [12]
Then was the noon-day glory clouded,
The sun in pitchy darkness shrouded.[13] 599
Then were strange forms through the darkness gleaming,
And the red orb of night on Jerusalem beaming;[14]

[1] 'Twas on that day, as
[2] mock'd   [3] 'Go! go!'
[4] he said,
[5] ,   [6] ;   [7] ,
[8] Nor see thy dying day
    Till I return again.'
[9] ,   [10] ;
[11] Hark that deep groan! He dies, he dies!   [12] !   [13] ;   [14] ,

Which faintly, with ensanguined light,
Dispersed the thickening shades of night.[1]
Convulsed, all nature shook with fear,
As if the very end was near; 605
Earth to her centre trembled;
Rent in twain was the temple's vail,
The graves gave up their dead; [2]
Whilst ghosts and spirits, ghastly pale,
Glared hideous on the sight, 610
Seen through the dark and lurid air,
As fiends array'd in light,
Threw on the scene a frightful glare,
And, howling, shriek'd with hideous yell—
They shriek'd in joy, for a Saviour fell! 615
'Twas then I felt the Almighty's ire;
Then full on my remembrance came
Those words despised alas! too late!
The horrors of my endless fate
Flashed on my soul and shook my frame; 620
They scorch'd my breast as with a flame
Of unextinguishable fire;
An exquisitely torturing pain

---

[1] ;
[2] The *Fraser* version here reads—
    Convulsed, all nature shook with fear,
    Earth trembled as if the end was near.
    Rent was the Temple's vail in twain—
    The graves gave up their dead again.

Of frenzying anguish fired my brain.[1]
By keen remorse and anguish driven, 625
I called for vengeance down from Heaven.
But, ah! the all-wasting hand of Time,
Might never wear away my crime!
I scarce could draw my fluttering breath—
Was it the appalling grasp of death? 630
I lay entranced, and deemed he shed
His dews of poppy o'er my head;
But though the kindly warmth was dead,
The self-inflicted torturing pangs
Of conscience lent their scorpion fangs, 635
Still life prolonging, after life was fled.

"Methought, what glories met my sight,
As burst a sudden blaze of light,
Illumining the azure skies,
I saw the blessed Saviour rise. 640
But how unlike to him who bled!
Where then his thorn-encircled head?
Where the big drops of agony
Which dimmed the lustre of his eye?
Or deathlike hue that overspread 645

---

[1] In the *Fraser* version these nine lines are represented by four only—
"'Twas then I felt the Almighty's ire—
Those words flashed on my soul, my frame,
Scorched breast and brain as with a flame
Of unextinguishable fire!

The features of that heavenly face?
Gone now was every mortal trace;
His eyes with radiant lustre beamed—
His form confessed celestial grace,
And with a blaze of glory streamed.   650
Innumerable hosts around,
Their brows with wreaths immortal crowned,
With amaranthine chaplets bound,
As on their wings the cross they bore,
Deep dyed in the Redeemer's gore,   655
Attune their golden harps, and sing
Loud hallelujahs to their King.

"But, in an instant, from my sight,
Fled were the visions of delight.
Darkness had spread her raven pall;   660
Dank, lurid darkness cover'd all.
All was as silent as the dead;
I felt a petrifying dread,
Which harrowed up my frame;
When suddenly a lurid stream   665
Of dark red light, with hideous gleam,
Shot like a meteor through the night,
And painted Hell upon the skies—
The Hell from whence it came.
What clouds of sulphur seemed to rise!   670
What sounds were borne upon the air!

The breathings of intense despair—
The piteous shrieks—the wails of woe—
The screams of torment and of pain—
The red-hot rack—the clanking chain ! 675
I gazed upon the gulf below,
Till, fainting from excess of fear,
My tottering knees refused to bear
My odious weight. I sink—I sink !
Already had I reached the brink. 680
The fiery waves disparted wide,
To plunge me in their sulphurous tide ;
When, racked by agonizing pain,
I started into life again.

"Yet still the impression left behind 685
Was deeply graven on my mind,
In characters whose inward trace
No change or time could e'er deface ;
A burning cross illumed my brow,
I hid it with a fillet grey, 690
But could not hide the wasting woe
That wore my wildered soul away,
And ate my heart with living fire.
I knew it was the avenger's sway,
I felt it was the avenger's ire ! 695

"A burden on the face of earth,

I cursed the mother who gave me birth ;
I cursed myself—my native land.
Polluted by repeated crimes,
I sought in distant foreign climes 700
If change of country could bestow
A transient respite from my woe.
Vain from myself the attempt to fly,
Sole cause of my own misery.

" Since when, in death-like trance I lay, 705
Past, slowly past, the years away
That poured a bitter stream on me,
When once I fondly longed to see
Jerusalem, alas ! my native place,
Jerusalem, alas ! no more in name, 710
No portion of her former fame
Had left behind a single trace.
Her pomp, her splendour, was no more.
Her towers no longer seem to rise,
To lift their proud heads to the skies. 715
Fane and monumental bust,
Long levelled even with the dust.
The holy pavements were stained with gore.
The place where the sacred temple stood
Was crimson-dyed with Jewish blood. 720
Long since, my parents had been dead,
All my posterity had bled

Beneath the dark Crusader's spear,
No friend was left my path to cheer,
To shed a few last setting rays   725
Of sunshine on my evening days!

" *Rack'd by the tortures of the mind,*
How have I long'd to plunge beneath
The mansions of repelling death !
And strove that resting place to find   730
Where earthly sorrows cease.
Oft, when the tempest-fiends engaged,
And the warring winds tumultuous raged,
Confounding skies with seas,
Then would I rush to the towering height   735
Of the gigantic Teneriffe,
Or some precipitous cliff,
All in the dead of the silent night.

" *I have cast myself from the mountain's height,*
Above was day—below was night;   740
The substantial clouds that lower'd beneath
Bore my detested form ;
They whirl'd it above the volcanic breath,
And the meteors of the storm ;
The torrents of electric flame   745
Scorch'd to a cinder my fated frame.
Hark to the thunder's awful crash—

Hark to the midnight lightning's hiss!
At length was heard a sullen dash,
Which made the hollow rocks around   750
Rebellow to the awful sound;
The yawning ocean opening wide,
Received me in its vast abyss,
And whelm'd me in its foaming tide.
Though my astounded senses fled,   755
Yet did the spark of life remain;
Then the wild surges of the main
Dash'd and left me on the rocky shore.
Oh! would that I had waked no more!
Vain wish! I lived again to feel   760
Torments more fierce than those of hell!
A tide of keener pain to roll,
And the bruises to enter my inmost soul![1]

[1] This passage, which, as given in the *Literary Journal*, consists of 37 lines, is represented in *Fraser* by 24 lines only:—

"How have I longed to plunge beneath
  The mansions of repelling death
  Where earthly sorrows cease!
Oft have I rushed to the towering height
  Of the gigantic Teneriffe,
  Or some precipitous cliff,
All in the dead of the stormy night,
  And flung me to the seas.
The substantial clouds that lower'd beneath,
  Bore my detested form;
They whirl'd it above volcanic breath,
  And the meteors of the storm.
Hark to the thunder's awful crash!
Hark to the midnight lightning's hiss!

"I cast myself in Etna's womb,[1]
If haply I might meet my doom,   765

    At length was heard a sullen dash,
    Which made the hollow rocks around
    Rebellow to the awful sound,
    The yawning ocean opening wide,
    Received me in its vast abyss,
    And whelm'd me in its foaming tide—
    My astounded senses fled !
    Oh ! would that I had waked no more,
    But the wild surge swept my corpse ashore—
    I was not with the dead !

[1] "I cast myself from the overhanging summit of the gigantic Teneriffe into the wide weltering ocean. The clouds which hung upon its base below, bore up my odious weight; the foaming billows swoln by the fury of the northern blast, opened to receive me, and, burying in a vast abyss, at length dashed my almost inanimate frame against the crags. The bruises entered into my soul, but I awoke to life and all its torments. I precipitated myself into the crater of Vesuvius, the bickering flames and melted lava vomited me up again and though I felt the tortures of the damned, though the sulphureous bitumen scorched the blood within my veins, parched up my flesh and burnt it to a cinder, still did I live to drag the galling chain of existence on. Repeatedly have I exposed myself to the tempestuous battling of the elements; the clouds which burst upon my head in crash terrific and exterminating, and the flaming thunderbolt hurled headlong on me its victim, stunned but not destroyed me. The lightning, in bickering coruscation, blasted me; and like the scattered [? shattered] oak, which remains a monument of faded grandeur, and outlives the other monarchs of the forest, doomed me to live for ever. Nine times did this dagger enter into my heart—the ensanguined tide of existence followed the repeated plunge; at each stroke, unutterable anguish seized my frame, and every limb was convulsed by the pangs of approaching dissolution. The wounds still closed, and still I breathe the hated breath of life."

    I have endeavoured to deviate as little as possible from the extreme sublimity of idea which the *style* of the German author, of which this is a translation, so forcibly impresses. [Author's note.]

In torrents of electric flame;
Thrice happy had I found a grave
'Mid fierce combustion's tumults dire,
'Mid oceans of volcanic fire
Which whirl'd me in their sulphurous wave,   770
And scorched to a cinder my hated frame,
Parch'd up the blood within my veins,
And rack'd my breast with damning pains;
Then hurl'd me from the mountain's entrails dread.
With what unutterable woe   775
Even now I feel this bosom glow—
I burn—I melt with fervent heat—
Again life's pulses wildly beat—
What endless throbbing pains I live to feel!
The elements respect their Maker's seal,—   780
That seal deep printed on my fated head.

"Still like the scathed pine-tree's height,
Braving the tempests of the night
Have I 'scaped the bickering fire.
Like the scathed pine which a monument stands   785
Of faded grandeur, which the brands
Of the tempest-shaken air
Have riven on the desolate heath,
Yet it stands majestic even in death,
And rears its wild form there.   790
Thus have I 'scaped the ocean's roar

The red-hot bolt from God's right hand,
The flaming midnight meteor brand,
And Etna's flames of bickering fire.
Thus am I doom'd by fate to stand, 795
A monument of the Eternal's ire;
Nor can this being pass away,
Till time shall be no more.

"I pierce with intellectual eye,
Into each hidden mystery; 800
I penetrate the fertile womb
Of nature; I produce to light
The secrets of the teeming earth,
And give air's unseen embryos birth:
The past, the present, and to come, 805
Float in review before my sight:
To me is known the magic spell,
To summon e'en the Prince of Hell;
Awed by the Cross upon my head,
His fiends would obey my mandates dread, 810
To twilight change the blaze of noon,
And stain with spots of blood the moon—
But that an interposing hand
Restrains my potent arts, my else supreme command."

He raised his passion-quivering hand, 815
He loosed the grey encircling band,

A burning Cross was there;
Its colour was like to recent blood,
Deep marked upon his brow it stood,
And spread a lambent glare.   820
Dimmer grew the taper's blaze,
Dazzled by the brighter rays,
Whilst Paulo spoke—'twas dead of night—
Fair Rosa shuddered with affright;
Victorio, fearless, had braved death   825
Upon the blood-besprinkled heath;
Had heard, unmoved, the cannon's roar,
Echoing along the Wolga's shore.
When the thunder of battle was swelling,
When the birds for their dead prey were yelling,   830
When the ensigns of slaughter were streaming,
And falchions and bayonets were gleaming,
And almost felt death's chilling hand,
Stretched on ensanguined Wolga's strand,
And, careless, scorned for life to cry,   835
Yet now he turned aside his eye,
Scarce could his death-like terror bear,
And owned now what it was to fear.

" Once a funeral met my aching sight,
It blasted my eyes at the dead of night,   840
When the sightless fiends of the tempests rave,
And hell-birds howl o'er the storm-blacken'd wave.

Nought was seen, save at fits, but the meteor's glare
And the lightnings of God painting hell on the air;
Nought was heard save the thunder's wild voice in the sky, 845
And strange birds who, shrieking, fled dismally by.
'Twas then from my head my drench'd hair that I tore,
And bade [1] my vain dagger's point drink my life's gore;
'Twas then I fell on the ensanguined earth,
And cursed the mother who gave me birth! 850
My maddened brain could bear no more—
Hark! the chilling whirlwind's roar;
The spirits of the tombless dead
Flit around my fated head,—
Howl horror and destruction round, 855
As they quaff my blood that stains the ground,
And shriek amid their deadly stave,—
' Never shalt thou find the grave!
Ever shall thy fated soul
In life's protracted torments roll, 860
Till, in latest ruin hurl'd,
And fate's destruction, sinks the world!
Till the dead arise from the yawning ground,
To meet their Maker's last decree,
Till angels of vengeance flit around, 865
And loud yelling demons seize on thee!'

[1] bid

"Ah! would were come that fated hour,
When the clouds of chaos around shall lower;
When this globe calcined by the fury of God
Shall sink beneath his wrathful nod!"

As thus he spake, a wilder gaze
Of fiend-like horror lit his eye
With a most unearthly blaze,
As if some phantom-form passed by.
At last he stilled the maddening wail
Of grief, and thus pursued his tale :—

"Oft I invoke the fiends of hell,
And summon each in dire array—
I know they dare not disobey
My stern, my powerful spell.
—Once on a night, when not a breeze
Ruffled the surface of the seas,
The elements were lulled to rest,
And all was calm save my sad breast,
On death resolved—intent,
I marked a circle round my form;
About me sacred reliques spread,
The reliques of magicians dead,
And potent incantations read—
I waited their event.

"All at once grew dark the night,
Mists of swarthiness hung o'er the pale moonlight.
Strange yells were heard, the boding cry
Of the night raven that flitted by,
Whilst the silver winged mew   895
Startled with screams o'er the dark wave flew.
'Twas then I seized a magic wand,
The wand by an enchanter given,
And deep dyed in his heart's red blood.
The crashing thunder pealed aloud;   900
I saw the portentous meteor's glare
And the lightnings gleam o'er the lurid air;
I raised the wand in my trembling hand,
And pointed Hell's mark at the zenith of Heaven.

"A superhuman sound   905
Broke faintly on the listening ear,
Like to a silver harp the notes,
And yet they were more soft and clear.
I wildly strained my eyes around—
Again the unknown music floats.   910
Still stood Hell's mark above my head—
In wildest accents I summoned the dead—
And through the unsubstantial night,
It diffused a strange and fiendish light;
Spread its rays to the charnel-house air, 915
And marked mystic forms on the dark vapours there.

The winds had ceased—a thick dark smoke
From beneath the pavement broke ;
Around ambrosial perfumes breathe
A fragrance, grateful to the sense,   920
And bliss, past utterance, dispense.
The heavy mists, encircling, wreath,
Disperse, and gradually unfold
A youthful female form ;—she rode
Upon a rosy-tinted cloud ;   925
Bright stream'd her flowing locks of gold ;
She shone with radiant lustre bright,
And blazed with strange and dazzling light ;
A diamond coronet deck'd her brow,
Bloom'd on her cheek a vermeil glow ;   930
The terrors of her fiery eye
Pour'd forth insufferable day,
And shed a wildly lurid ray.
A smile upon her features play'd,
But there, too, sate pourtray'd   935
The inventive malice of a soul
Where wild demoniac passions roll ;
Despair and torment on her brow,
Had mark'd a melancholy woe
In dark and deepen'd shade.   940
Under those hypocritic smiles,
Deceitful as the serpent's wiles,
Her hate and malice were conceal'd ;

Whilst on her guilt-confessing face,
Conscience, the strongly printed trace 945
Of agony betray'd,
And all the fallen angel stood reveal'd.
She held a poniard in her hand,
The point was tinged by the lightning's brand;
In her left a scroll she bore, 950
Crimson'd deep with human gore;
And, as above my head she stood,
Bade me smear it with my blood.
She said, that when it was my doom
That every earthly pang should cease; 955
The evening of my mortal woe
Would close beneath the yawning tomb;
And, lull'd into the arms of death,
I should resign my labouring breath;
And in the sightless realms below 960
Enjoy an endless reign of peace.
She ceased—oh, God, I thank thy grace,
Which bade me spurn the deadly scroll;
Uncertain for a while I stood—
The dagger's point was in my blood. 965
Even now I bleed!—I bleed!
When suddenly what horrors flew,
Quick as the lightnings through my frame;
Flash'd on my mind the infernal deed,
The deed which would condemn my soul 970

To torments of eternal flame.
Drops colder than the cavern dew
Quick coursed each other down my face,
I labour'd for my breath;
At length I cried, 'Avaunt! thou fiend of Hell,   975
Avaunt! thou minister of death!'
I cast the volume on the ground,
Loud shriek'd the fiend with piercing yell,
And more than mortal laughter peal'd around.
The scatter'd fragments of the storm   980
Floated along the Demon's form,
Dilating till it touched the sky;
The clouds that roll'd athwart his eye,
Reveal'd by its terrific ray,
Brilliant as the noontide day,   985
Gleam'd with a lurid fire;
Red lightnings darted around his head,
Thunders hoarse as the groans of the dead,
Pronounced their Maker's ire;
A whirlwind rush'd impetuous by,   990
Chaos of horror fill'd the sky;
I sunk convulsed with awe and dread.
When I waked the storm was fled,
But sounds unholy met my ear,
And fiends of hell were flitting near.   995

"Here let me pause—here end my tale,

My mental powers begin to fail;
At this short retrospect I faint:
Scarce beats my pulse—I lose my breath,
I sicken even unto death.   1000
Oh! hard would be the task to paint
And gift with life past scenes again;
To knit a long and linkless chain,
Or strive minutely to relate
The varied horrors of my fate.   1005
Rosa! I could a tale disclose,
So full of horror—full of woes,
Such as might blast a demon's ear,
Such as a fiend might shrink to hear—
But, no—"   1010

Here ceased the tale. Convulsed with fear,
The tale yet lived in Rosa's ear—
She felt a strange mysterious dread,
A chilling awe as of the dead;
Gleamed on her sight the demon's form.   1015
Heard she the fury of the storm?
The cries and hideous yells of death?
Tottered the ground her feet beneath?
Was it the fiend before her stood?
Saw she the poniard drop with blood?   1020
All seemed to her distempered eye
A true and sad reality

   *   *   *   *   *

CANTO IV.

Οὕτοι, γυναῖκας, ἀλλὰ Γοργόνας λέγω·
ὐδ' αὖτε Γοργείοισιν εἰκάσω τύποις·
—— μέλαιναι δ' ἐς τὸ πᾶν βδελύκτροποι·
ῥέγκουσι δ' οὐ πλατοῖσι φυσιάμασιν·
ἐκ δ' ὀμμάτων λείβουσι δυσφιλῆ βίαν.
Æschylus, Eumenides, v. 48.

" —— What are ye
So withered and so wild in your attire,
That look not like th' inhabitants of earth,
And yet are on't?—Live you, or are you aught
That man may question?" *Macbeth.*

AH! why does man, whom God has sent
As the Creation's ornament,
Who stands amid his works confest   1025
The first—the noblest—and the best;
Whose vast—whose comprehensive eye,
Is bounded only by the sky,
O'erlook the charms which Nature yields,
The garniture of woods and fields,   1030
The sun's all vivifying light,
The glory of the moon by night,

And to himself alone a foe,
Forget from whom these blessings flow?
And is there not in friendship's eye, 1035
Beaming with tender sympathy,
An antidote to every woe?[1]
And cannot woman's love bestow
An heav'nly paradise below?
Such joys as these to man are given, 1040
And yet you dare to rail at Heaven;[2]
Vainly oppose the Almighty Cause,
Transgress His universal laws;[3]
Forfeit the pleasures that await
The virtuous in this mortal state;[4] 1045
Question the goodness of the Power on high,
In misery live, despairing die.
What then is man, how few his days,
And heighten'd by what transient rays;[5]
Made up of plans of happiness, 1050
Of visionary schemes of bliss,
The varying passions of his mind
Inconstant, varying as the wind;[6]
Now hush'd to apathetic rest,
Now tempested with storms his breast;[7] 1055
Now with the fluctuating tide
Sunk low in meanness, swoln with pride;[8]

[1], [2], [3], [4], [5], [6], [7], [8]

Thoughtless, or overwhelm'd with care,
Hoping, or tortured by despair!

The sun had sunk beneath the hill, 1060
Soft fell the dew, the scene was still;
All nature hailed the evening's close.
Far more did lovely Rosa bless
The twilight of her happiness.
Even Paulo blest the tranquil hour 1065
As in the aromatic bower,
Or wandering through the olive grove,
He told his plaintive tale of love;
But welcome to Victorio's soul
Did the dark clouds of evening roll! 1070
But, ah! what means his hurried pace,
Those gestures strange, that varying face;
Now pale with mingled rage and ire,
Now burning with intense desire;
That brow where brood the imps of care, 1075
That fixed expression of despair,
That haste, that labouring for breath—
His soul is madly bent on death.
A dark resolve is in his eye,
Victorio raves—I hear him cry, 1080
" Rosa is Paulo's eternally."

But whence is that soul-harrowing moan,
Deep drawn and half supprest—

A low and melancholy tone,
That rose upon the wind ?   1085
Victorio wildly gazed around,
He cast his eyes upon the ground,
He raised them to the spangled air,
But all was still—was quiet there.
Hence, hence, this superstitious fear ;   1090
'Twas but the fever of his mind,
That conjured the ideal sound,
To his distempered ear.

With rapid step, with frantic haste,
He scoured the long and dreary waste ;   1095
And now the gloomy cypress spread
Its darkened umbrage o'er his head ;
The stately pines above him high,
Lifted their tall heads to the sky ;
Whilst o'er his form, the poisonous yew   1100
And melancholy nightshade threw
Their baleful deadly dew.
At intervals the moon shone clear ;
Yet, passing o'er her disk, a cloud
Would now her silver beauty shroud.   1105
The autumnal leaf was parched and sere ;
It rustled like a step to fear.
The precipice's battled height
Was dimly seen through the mists of night,

As Victorio moved along.	1110
At length he reach'd its summit dread,
The night-wind whistled round his head
A wild funereal song.
A dying cadence swept around
Upon the waste of air,	1115
It scarcely might be called a sound,
For stillness yet was there,
Save when the roar of the waters below
Was wafted by fits to the mountain's brow.
Here for a while Victorio stood	1120
Suspended o'er[1] the yawning flood,
And gazed upon the gulf beneath.
No apprehension paled his cheek,
No sighs from his torn bosom break,
No terror dimm'd his eye.	1125
" Welcome, thrice welcome, friendly death,"
In desperate harrowing tone he cried,
" Receive me, ocean, to your breast,
Hush this ungovernable tide,
This troubled sea to rest.	1130
Thus do I bury all my grief—
This plunge shall give my soul relief,
This plunge into eternity!"
I see him now about to spring

[1] On

Into the watery grave: 1135
Hark! the death angel flaps his wing
O'er the blacken'd wave.
Hark! the night-raven shrieks on high
To the breeze which passes on ;
Clouds o'ershade the moonlight sky— 1140
The deadly work is almost done—
When a soft and silver sound,
Softer than the fairy song,
Which floats at midnight hour along
The daisy-spangled ground, 1145
Was borne upon the wind's soft swell.
Victorio started—'twas the knell
Of some departed soul ;
Now on the pinion of the blast,
Which o'er the craggy mountain past, 1150
The lengthen'd murmurs roll—
Till lost in ether, dies away
The plaintive, melancholy lay.
'Tis said congenial sounds have power
To dissipate the mists that lower 1155
Upon the wretch's brow—
To still the maddening passions' war—
To calm the mind's impetuous jar—
To turn the tide of woe.
Victorio shudder'd with affright, 1160
Swam o'er his eyes thick mists of night;

Even now he was about to sink
Into the ocean's yawning womb,
But that the branches of an oak,
Which, riven by the lightning's stroke,   1165
O'erhung the precipice's brink,
Preserved him from the billowy tomb;
Quick throbb'd his pulse with feverish heat,
He wildly started on his feet,
And rush'd from the mountain's height.   1170

The moon was down, but thro' the air
Wild meteors spread a transient glare,
Borne on the wing of the swelling gale,
Above the dark and woody dale,
Thick clouds obscured the sky.   1175
All was now wrapped in silence drear,
Not a whisper broke on the listening ear,
Not a murmur floated by.

In thought's perplexing labyrinth lost
The trackless heath he swiftly crost.   1180
Ah! why did terror blanch his cheek?
Why did his tongue attempt to speak,
And fail in the essay?
Through the dark midnight mists, an eye,
Flashing with crimson brilliancy,   1185
Poured on his face its ray.

What sighs pollute the midnight air?
What mean those breathings of despair?
Thus asked a voice, whose hollow tone
Might seem but one funereal moan.   1190
Victorio groaned, with faltering breath,
"I burn with love, I pant for death!"

Suddenly a meteor's glare,
With brilliant flash illumed the air;
Bursting through clouds of sulphurous smoke,   1195
As on a Witch's form it broke,
Of herculean bulk her frame
Seemed blasted by the lightning's flame;
Her eyes that flared with lurid light,
Were now with bloodshot lustre filled.   1200
They blazed like comets through the night,
And now thick rheumy gore distilled;
Black as the raven's plume, her locks
Loose streamed upon the pointed rocks;
Wild floated on the hollow gale,   1205
Or swept the ground in matted trail;
Vile loathsome weeds, whose pitchy fold
Were blackened by the fire of Hell,
Her shapeless limbs of giant mould
Scarce served to hide—as she the while   1210
"Grinned horribly a ghastly smile"
And shrieked with demon yell. .

Terror unmanned Victorio's mind,
His limbs, like lime leaves in the wind,
Shook, and his brain in wild dismay   1215
Swam—Vainly he strove to turn away.
" Follow me to the mansions of rest,"
The weird female cried ;
The life-blood rushed thro' Victorio's breast
In full and swelling tide.   1220
Attractive as the eagle's gaze,
And bright as the meridian blaze,
Led by a sanguine stream of light,
He followed through the shades of night—
Before him his conductress fled,   1225
As swift as the ghosts of the dead,
When on some dreadful errand they fly,
In a thunderblast sweeping the sky.

They reached a rock whose beetling height
Was dimly seen thro' the clouds of night ;   1230
Illumined by the meteor's blaze,
Its wild crags caught the reddened rays
And their refracted brilliance threw
Around a solitary yew,
Which stretched its blasted form on high, 1235
Braving the tempests of the sky.
As glared the flame—a caverned cell,
More pitchy than the shades of hell,

Lay open to Victorio's view.
Lost for an instant was his guide ; 1240
He rushed into the mountain's side.
At length with deep and harrowing yell
She bade him quickly speed,
For that ere again had risen the moon
'Twas fated that there must be done 1245
A strange—a deadly deed.

Swift as the wind Victorio sped;
Beneath him lay the mangled dead
Around dank putrefaction's power
Had caused a dim blue mist to lower. 1250
Yet an unfixed, a wandering light
Dispersed the thickening shades of night;
Yet the weird female's features dire
Gleamed thro' the lurid yellow air:
With a deadly livid fire, 1255
Whose wild, inconstant, dazzling light
Dispelled the tenfold shades of night,
Whilst her hideous fiendlike eye
Fixed on her victim with horrid stare
Flamed with more kindled radiancy; 1260
More frightful far than that of Death,
When exulting he stalks o'er the battle heath;
Or of the dread prophetic form,
Who rides the curled clouds in the storm,

And borne upon the tempest's wings,   1265
Death, despair, and horror brings.
Strange voices then and shrieks of death
Were borne along the trackless heath;
Tottered the ground his steps beneath;
Rustled the blast o'er the dark cliff's side,   1270
And their works unhallowed spirits plied,
As they shed their baneful breath.

Yet Victorio hastened on—
Soon the dire deed will be done.
"Mortal," the female cried, "this night   1275
Shall dissipate thy woe;
And, ere return of morning light
The clouds that shade thy brow,
Like fleeting summer mists shall fly
Before the sun that mounts on high.   1280
I know the wishes of thy heart—
A soothing balm I could impart:
Rosa is Paulo's—can be thine,
For the secret power is mine."

VICTORIO.

"Give me that secret power—Oh! give   1285
To me fair Rosa—I will live
To bow to thy command.
Rosa but mine—and I will fly

E'en to the regions of the sky,
Will traverse every land."   1290

WITCH.

" Calm then those transports and attend,
Mortal, to one, who is thy friend—
The charm begins."

            An ancient book
Of mystic characters she took;
Her loose locks floated on the air;[1]   1295
Her eyes were fixed in lifeless stare:[2]
She traced a circle on the floor,
Around dank chilling vapours lower:[3]
A golden cross on the pavement she threw,[4]
'Twas tinged with[5] a flame of lambent blue,   1300
From which bright scintillations flew;[6]
By it she cursed her Saviour's soul;[7]
Around strange fiendish laughs did roll,
A hollow, wild, and frightful sound,
At fits was heard to float around.[8]   1305
She uttered[9] then, in accents dread,
Some maddening rhyme that wakes the dead,

---

[1] ,   [2] ;   [3] ;   [4] ;   [5] by   [6] ;—   [7] !—
[8] Then savage laughter round did roll,
    A hollow, wild, and frightful sound,
    In air above, and under ground.
[9] utter'd.

And forces every shivering fiend,
To her their demon-forms to bend;[1]
At length a wild and piercing shriek,
As the dark mists disperse and break,
Announced the coming Prince of Hell—[2]
His horrid form obscured the cell.
Victorio shrunk, unused to shrink,
E'en at extremest danger's brink;
The witch then pointed to the ground,
Infernal shadows flitted around,
And with their prince were seen to rise,
The cavern bellows with their cries,
Which echoing through a thousand caves,
Sound like as many tempest waves.[3]

Inspired and wrapt in bickering flame,

[1] .   [2] !

[3] This passage differs considerably from the *Literary Journal* version:—

    But when his form obscured the cell,
    What words could paint, what tongue could tell,
    The terrors of his look!
    The witch's heart unused to shrink
    Even at extremest danger's brink,
    With deadliest terror shook!
    And with their Prince were seen to rise
    Spirits of every shape and hue,—
    A hideous and infernal crew,
    With hell-fires flashing from their eyes.
    The cavern bellows with their cries,
    Which, echoing through a thousand caves,
    Sound like as many tempest-waves.

The strange, the awful being stood.¹
Words unpremeditated came,
In unintelligible flood,   1325
From her black tumid lips,²—array'd
In livid fiendish smiles of joy;³
Lips, which now dropped⁴ with deadly dew,
And now, extending wide, displayed,⁵
Projecting teeth of mouldy hue,⁶   1330
As with a loud and piercing cry,
A mystic, harrowing lay she sang,
Along the rocks a death-peal rang.
In accents hollow, deep and drear,
They struck upon Victorio's ear.⁷   1335
As ceased the soul-appalling verse,
Obedient to its power, grew still
The hellish shrieks;—the mists disperse;—
Satan—a shapeless, hideous beast—
In all his horrors stood confest!   1340
And as his vast proportions fill
The lofty cave, his features dire
Gleam with a pale and sulphurous fire;
From his fixed glance of deadly hate

---

¹ The strange and wild enchantress stood;—
² —   ³ —   ⁴ dropp'd   ⁵ display'd
⁶ blue.
⁷ The rocks, as with a death-peal, rang
  And the dread accents, deep and drear,
  Struck terror on the dark night's ear!

Even she *shrunk back, appalled with dread—* 1345
For there contempt and malice sate,
And from his basiliskine eye
Sparks of living fury fly,
Which wanted but a being to strike dead.
A wilder, a more awful spell 1350
Now echoed through the long-drawn cell;
The demon bowed to its mandates dread.
"Receive this potent drug," he cried,
"Whoever quaffs its fatal tide,
Is mingled with the dead." 1355
Swept by a rushing sulphurous blast,
Which wildly through the cavern past,
The fatal word was borne.
The cavern trembled with the sound,[1]
Trembled beneath his feet the ground, 1360
With strong convulsions torn,
Victorio, shuddering, fell;
But soon awakening from his trance,
He cast around a fearful glance,
Yet gloomy was the cell, 1365
Save where a lamp's uncertain flare
Cast a flickering, dying glare.

---

[1] "Death!
Hell trembled at the hideous name and sighed
From all its caves, and back resounded death."—*Paradise Lost.*

WITCH.

"Receive this dear-earned drug—its power
Thou, mortal, soon shalt know:
This drug shall be thy nuptial dower,   1370
This drug shall seal thy woe.
Mingle it with Rosa's wine,
Victorio—Rosa then is thine."

She spake, and, to confirm the spell,
A strange and subterranean sound   1375
Reverberated long around,
In dismal echoes—the dark cell
Rocked as in terror—thro' the sky
Hoarse thunders murmured awfully,
And winged with horror, darkness spread   1380
Her mantle o'er Victorio's head.
He gazed around with dizzy fear,
No fiend, no witch, no cave, was near;
But the blasts of the forest were heard to roar,
The wild ocean's billows to dash on the shore.   1385
The cold winds of Heaven struck chill on his frame;
For the cave had been heated by hell's blackening flame,
And his hand grasped a casket—the philtre was there!

    *   *   *   *   *

Sweet is the whispering of the breeze
Which scarcely sways yon summer trees;   1390

Sweet is the pale moon's pearly beam,
Which sleeps upon the silver stream,
In slumber cold and still:
Sweet those wild notes of harmony,
Which on the blast that passes by,   1395
Are wafted from yon hill;
So low, so thrilling, yet so clear,
Which strike enthusiast fancy's ear:
Which sweep along the moonlight sky,
Like notes of heavenly symphony.   1400

SONG.

See yon opening flower
Spreads its fragrance to the blast;
It fades within an hour,
Its decay is pale, is fast.
Paler is yon maiden;   1405
Faster is her heart's decay;
Deep with sorrow laden,
She sinks in death away.

   *   *   *   *   *

'Tis the silent dead of night—
Hark! hark! what shriek so low yet clear,   1410
Breaks on calm rapture's pensive ear,
From Lara's castled height?
'Twas Rosa's death-shriek fell!
What sound is that which rides the blast,

As onward its fainter murmurs past ? 1415
'Tis Rosa's funeral knell !
What step is that the ground which shakes ?
'Tis the step of a wretch, nature shrinks from his tread;
And beneath their tombs tremble the shuddering dead;
And while he speaks the churchyard quakes. 1420

PAULO.

"*Lies she there for the worm to devour,*
Lies she there till the judgment hour,
Is then my Rosa dead !
False fiend ! I curse thy futile power !
O'er her form will lightnings flash, 1425
O'er her form will thunders crash,
But harmless from my head
Will the fierce tempest's fury fly,
Rebounding to its native sky.—
Who is the God of Mercy ?—where 1430
Enthroned the power to save ?
Reigns he above the viewless air ?
Lives he beneath the grave ?
To him would I lift my suppliant moan,
That power should hear my harrowing groan ;— 1435
Is it then Christ's terrific Sire ?
Ah ! I have felt his burning ire,
I feel,—I feel it now,—
His flaming mark is fix'd on my head,

And must there remain in traces dread ;   1440
Wild anguish glooms my brow ;
Oh ! Griefs like mine that fiercely burn,
Where is the balm can heal !
Where is the monumental urn
Can bid to dust this frame return,   1445
Or quench the pangs I feel !"
As thus he spoke grew dark the sky,
Hoarse thunders murmured awfully,
" O Demon ! I am thine !" he cried.
A hollow fiendish voice replied,   1450
" Come ! for thy doom is misery."[1]

---

[1] The *Fraser* version of the final section differs materially from that given above. I add it therefore for purposes of comparison :—

PAULO.

" Lies she there for the worm to devour ?
Lies she there till the judgment hour ?
Is then my Rosa dead ?
False fiend ! I curse thy futile power !
O'er her form will lightnings flash,
O'er her form will thunders crash,
But harmless from my head
Will the fierce tempest's fury fly,
Rebounding to its native sky.
Who is the God of Mercy ?—where
Enthrones the power to save ?
Reigns he above the viewless air ?
Lives he beneath the grave ?
To him would I lift my suppliant moan,
That power should hear my harrowing groan ;
Is it then Christ's terrific Sire ?
Ah ! I have felt his burning ire,—

F

Wild anguish glooms my brow ;
His flaming mark is fixed on my head,
And must there remain in traces dread ;
I feel—I feel it now !"

As thus he spoke grew dark the sky,
Hoarse thunders murmured awfully,
"O Demon ! I am thine !" he cried,
A hollow, fiendish voice replied,
"Come ! for thy doom is **misery** !"

APPENDIX.

THE WANDERING JEW'S SOLILOQUY.

Is it the Eternal Triune, is it He
Who dares arrest the wheels of destiny
And plunge me in the lowest Hell of Hells?
Will not the lightning's blast destroy my frame?
Will not steel drink the blood-life where it swells?
No—let me hie where dark Destruction dwells,
To rouse her from her deeply caverned lair,
And taunting her curst sluggishness to ire
Light long Oblivion's death torch at its flame
And calmly mount Annihilation's pyre.

Tyrant of Earth! pale misery's jackal thou!
Are there no stores of vengeful violent fate
Within the magazines of thy fierce hate?
No poison in the clouds to bathe a brow
That lowers on thee with desperate contempt?
Where is the noonday pestilence that slew
The myriad sons of Israel's favoured nation?
Where the destroying minister that flew

Pouring the fiery tide of desolation
Upon the leagued Assyrian's attempt?
Where the dark Earthquake demon who ingorged
At the dread word Korah's unconscious crew?
Or the Angel's two-edged sword of fire that urged
Our primal parents from their bower of bliss
(Reared by thine hand) for errors not their own
By Thine omniscient mind foredoomed, foreknown?
Yes! I would court a ruin such as this,
Almighty Tyrant! and give thanks to Thee—
Drink deeply—drain the cup of hate—remit this I may die.

[I have to thank C. J. E. Esdaile, Esq., for permission to publish the above poem, which now appears in print for the first time.]

INTRODUCTORY ARTICLE:

Prefixed to " The Wandering Jew" as published in
FRASER'S MAGAZINE.[1]

"MANKIND," says Quinctilian, speaking of the freedom and boldness of speech which often characterise the unlearned orator, "have a pleasure in hearing what they themselves are unwilling to say." Judging from its rarity it would seem that such candour occasions at times extremely unpleasant effects to the ingenuous speakers, who are consequently daily decreasing in number. The Frenchman who averred that if he had in his hand all the truths in the world, he would only open one finger at a time, made a bold avowal—there are numbers to whom it would be dangerous to open that one; for many are the Pilates who ask what is truth, yet are unfit to hear it. Unfortunately this extensive appetite, for which the world has so long been distinguished, has never had

[1] This article is printed here rather on account of its intrinsic interest, than because of its slight references to *The Wandering Jew.*

an opportunity of being gratified regarding the celebrated poet, whose works form the subject of our present reflections. The able and willing author, who well knew the calumnies of Mr. Shelley's enemies, though he had every desire to render justice to his genius, and leave to posterity a token that his elevated and unearthly mind was understood by at least one generous contemporary, having fairly weighed his philosophy in the balance and found it wanting, therefore dealt out just that meed of faint praise which amounts to the acknowledgment that a defence is no longer tenable. By the opposite Aristarchus, who defended the party of optimists in religion, philosophy, and politics, advantage was taken of youthful errors, in after life devoutly retracted, to insinuate the existence of opinions and morals perfectly at variance with the well-being of society, and to brand, with the mark of Cain, the brow of one whose life shewed, by the most unequivocal demonstration, that instead of being an atheistical anarch, he was pious towards nature, towards his friends, towards the whole human race, towards the meanest insect of the forest; in a word, that he loved every thing that was nature's and was untainted by man's misery. We cannot sufficiently express our regret at the charity of those men who, living in the way they see others live, without regard to the mode being right or wrong, could describe to the world as the unprincipled enemy of morality a man who from the cradle to the grave was weighed down by the burden of an anxiety for the future, ever held before his eyes by a weak and consumptive constitution; who, elevated by a great prevailing sentiment into the highest regions of the moral world, passed his days in a passionate straining after a solution of the "Mystery of God," the great mystery of his suffering vice and confusion to prevail; and who, guided by a philosophy of life [1] which would be unanswerable in its conclusions were it possible to assume as a rule of life, pure and strict justice without reference to the collateral affections of man, endeavoured to reconcile together his life and his aspirations after human perfectibility. A time, however, has at last come, when, without danger, an admission of such a truth may be made. The remorseless deep has closed over the head of Lycidas, and the friends whom he loved may now bid his brave and gentle spirit repose, for the human beings whom he laboured for begin to know him. He must not float unwept upon his watery bier, because his admirers are voiceless and tuneless; nor must enmity be allowed through ignorance to extend beyond the funeral pyre, in a land where men are still just, and pity is of ancient date.

"Oltre il rogo non vive ira nemica,
 E nell' ospite suolo ove io ti lasso,
 Giuste son l'alme, e la pietade è antica."
Monti's *Basvigliana*.

To distinguish the true poet from the mere hunter after

[1] Godwin's *Political Justice;*—for the analysis of which, see the character of its author in the *Spirit of the Age*.

images and conceits, the talent of producing rhetorical phraseology, and turning smooth verses, however trivial and devoid of ideas the mode of feeling, judging, and imagining may be, it is necessary that he should be endowed with a creative genius, be initiated in the deep mystery of the harmony of nature and the human mind, and gifted with an infallible instinct of the beautiful, that rejects every impure or incongruous element, now giving a "local habitation and a name" to invisible things, now emerging from the etherial, and exalting to heaven the terrestrial.—The study and profound contemplation of which masters will shew that poetry is the re-produced, clear, and intimate mingling of the visible and invisible worlds, the rhythm and measure of every life, the original form of the soul, or in whatever other manner we may describe that divine gift conceded to those few who are born the depositaries and mirrors of the intellectual treasures of an age.

The proper business of art is to represent only the eternal, viz., that which is at all places, and in all times significant and beautiful; but this cannot be done without the intervention of a veil. Upon the choice of this veil depends the character of the artist. If, like Shakspeare, he describe the riddle of human life, his is the poetry of society, the *jucunda et idonea vitæ*, to use Horace's words; if, like Milton, he pursue the infinite, it is the poetry of abstraction. He draws less upon our social sympathies, yet, though he do himself the injustice to choose subjects which he could never adequately describe, he may yet be honoured as a poet of the first class; for he also founds upon an intuitive sense, from which all philosophy of life and true feeling are derivative, that sense of the eternal and beautiful which centres in religion. To point out to man wherein consists this highest life, is alike the object of both. In all poets who have been eminently the poets of intellect this progress of the mind to abstraction is thus inevitable. They create a world of their own. The true poet seems then all-knowing, or, as it were, a world in miniature; and the last and deepest observers still find in him new harmonies with the infinite structure of the universe;—concurrences with later ideas, and affinities with the higher powers and senses of man. Thus there is, blindly woven through the web of our being, a principle which burns bright or dim, as each of us are mirrors of that fire of love and immortality for which all unceasingly thirst. If this foundation of nature's creating—this natural form or eternal identity of the individual, (if we may so call it,) be mysterious and impenetrable in the meanest human being, how much less can we pretend to unveil the mystery of a mind so highly endowed. It will be sufficient to have slightly indicated the concourse of the conflicting elements of his time, the tension of his own peculiar ones and their results.

If in comparing the chances of immortality to the greatest poets of our time, we assume as a test our theory that the writer who is the truest reflex of the feelings of his age, will be preferred by posterity, in opposition to the notion that it will be the one who depicts a character possessing a power of appealing to certain immutable feelings of mankind, independent of those of his age, we would suggest that the searching mind of modern Europe, its advanced state of science and politics, and its new mode of reviewing antiquity, are more vividly shadowed forth in Mr. Shelley's poetry than in that of his rival Byron. The French Revolution, that voice

"Which was the echo of three thousand years,"

and the various theories of morals and government, which, like the wild dreams of astrology, were agitated for the perfection of man, are there recorded as in a faithful mirror; but, from their extremes, defeat their object by disgusting the majority, and thereby giving their enemies additional power to continue the same round " which the weary world has ever ran;" at the same time souring the mind of the author into the desponding belief that it is not his own philanthropy that is defective in judgment, but the blindness of a hopeless world.

"Ma el mondo cieco che' el virtu non cura."

It is strange that a genius of such a rare and etherial order should not have perceived that to the eloquent but specious reasoning of Mirabaud, the Materialism of the *Système de la Nature*, so unanswerable to the matter-of-fact mind, there could not be given a better reply than by pointing to his own *Prometheus Unbound*. All is folly except the care bestowed on our existence—if we choose to think so. True poetry is indeed the best practical refutation of the maxim that there is nothing in the intellect that was not first in the senses, and of all the sorrowful deductions therefrom. Shelley's *Witch of Atlas*, his terrific *Triumph of Life*, or that most exquisite poem called *Epipsychidion*, which in the expression of exalted and Platonic love, rivals the *Triumphs* of Petrarch, or the *Vita Nuova* of Dante, surely give evidence of something inconceivably more delicate than a mere conjunction of external imagery.

"More subtle web Arachne cannot spin."

And so far are we from reducing the mind of man to a wonderful machine, that on perusing the works of Keats and Shelley, the countless combinations which appear so foreign to the mind of an indweller of a city, like the former, and the exceeding sympathy with nature displayed in the writings of the latter, almost incline us to be of Plato's pleasant belief, that all knowledge is but remembrance of a prior existence, relumed in us by the concords of poetry, the original form of the soul.

> "A cuyo son divino
> El alma que en olvido esta sumida
> Torna a cobrar el tino
> Y memoria perdida
> De su origen primera esclarecida."
> LUIS DE LEON.

That fantastic spirit which would bind all existence in

the visionary chain of intellectual beauty, and the forced and distorted tenor of such a philosophy, became in Shelley the centre in which his whole intellectual and sensitive powers were united for its formation and embellishment. And although in painting the romance, the conceits and the diversities, the workings and meanderings of a heart penetrated with such an ideal passion, drawing less upon our individual sympathies than on those of social life, he may be liable to the charge of a certain mannerism, there is not the less evident, the delicacy, elasticity, and concentration of a gentle and noble mind, a deep scorn of all that is vulgar and base, a lofty enthusiasm for liberty and the glory of his country, for science and for letters; and finally, an insatiable longing after an eternal and incorruptible being which opposed to his persuasion of the misery and nullity of this world, feeds and maintains that tension, or struggle, that "fire at the core" which is the inheritance of all privileged geniuses, the promoters of their age. Hence that restlessness coupled with the desire of repose, that ambition and vanity coupled with the disdain of worldly things, that retirement and misanthropy joined to benevolence, and the yearning after love and affection, the pursuit of fame, and the intolerance of contemporary criticism in conjunction with real and unaffected modesty; and in fine, that contrast of virtue and weakness which is the inheritance of flesh, so requisite, seemingly, to level the more sublime capacity with its fellow creatures, and to inculcate the religious bond of union which Christian charity ought to inspire. Hence, too, that querulous monotony, that desire in a tender soul of exiling itself from a world deprived of the projective power, and its relapse into its own void and indistinct generalities. Love is his deity, Plato his high-priest, Aristotle his sacristan, the poets leaders and composers of his choir, and the world a court of love or a floral game.

Yet there is something pathetic in this fragrant flower, so transitory seemingly in its essence and beauty. It is a delicate Ariel that would fain continue a little longer on the earth when the rays of Aurora and the approach of the living oblige it to vanish. Dismayed by the desert with which it is surrounded it passes through the universe and finds no associate or resting place for the sole of its foot. This divine emanation hears no responsive echo in nature, and the vulgar regard as folly that restlessness of soul which seems to want breathing room in the world for its enthusiasm and hope. A fatality is suspended over exalted souls, over those poets *che avrano intelletto di amore*, whose imagination depends on the faculty of loving and suffering.

> " Io mi son un che quando
> Amor mi spira noto ed in quel modo,
> Che ditta dentro vo significando."—DANTE.

As Madame de Staël says, "they are the exiles of another religion." "What," says the eloquent Corinne, " did the ancients mean when they spoke of destiny with so much terror ? What influence could that destiny have over the unvarying existence of common and tranquil beings ? They follow the changes of the seasons, they pass unruffled through the ordinary course of life, but the priestess who delivered the oracles was agitated by an awful power." There is, indeed, a woe too deep for tears when a surpassing spirit, whose light might have adorned the world, is warped from its native bias, leaving to friends behind it only despair and cold tranquillity, the web of nature and the tangled frame of human things, that to them are no longer what they once were. Ungrateful mortals do not feel their loss, and the gap it makes seems to close as quickly over his memory as the murderous sea over his living frame. The sacred rivers of righteousness and justice have rolled back upon their sources, and all things in this world seem plainly to go amiss.

How deeply expressive are those tender words of Euripides :—

> ἄνω ποταμῶν ἱερῶν χωροῦσι παγαί,
> καὶ δίκα καὶ πάντα πάλιν στρέφεται.
> ἀνδράσι μὲν δόλιαι βουλαί· θεῶν δ'
> οὐκέτι πίστις ἄραρε.

On the other hand, Byron, gifted with a stronger intellect though less fancy, and opposed to the visions and theories which in Shelley sometimes strike from their obscure grandeur, and at other times look like the dance and confusion of forms seen in a revolving kaleidoscope, is like Alfieri, stern, brief and succinct in his style, greatly inferior in stately and harmonious diction; but, nevertheless, more impressive from the direct appeal to our individual sympathies. In which particular Keats, not being troubled with much philosophy, is perhaps the superior of Shelley in spite of his negligent versification and mawkish sensibility. Byron gives us only the world of reality: Shelley that of desire. In examining the world the former views it as the difference between man and man; the latter as the difference between man and his Creator; thus presenting the metamorphosis of the human mind, and its progress from a sensual to an intellectual state. The one is full of that romance of monarchy and lordly chivalry which glosses over blood and the tears of human affections, by which the temple of the Moloch has been cemented, offering as compensation the gratification of passion and the glory and honour of this life to cheat the deluded victim. The other has the majestic spirit of antiquity, to which the world of debased Christianity and feudalism bears no reference, and is filled with a philosophy of liberty and equality drawn from the "fountains pure, nigh overgrown and lost," of Plato and the Greek tragedians, and the difference between man and man is regarded with the calm indifference of an extensive social system, which does not disdain to regard unless the greatest of heroes, of catastrophes and of geniuses, but is content to view the harmony of the whole. The one lived the life of a voluptuary, the other that of a hermit. Byron is the greater poet, Shelley the greater philanthropist; and he too had his temptations in the way of birth. The heir of an ancient Baronetcy and the representative of Sir Philip Sidney could forget this, refuse a seat in parliament, walk the hospitals for the benefit of the poor, and live a Pythagorean; all for the sake of a theory of man's perfectibility. But Byron's death in the cause of freedom cancelled all.

"Carminibus confide bonis: jacet ecce Tibullus!"—OVID.

With an apology for obtruding a fanciful and perhaps irrelevant comparison, we would submit that there appears to us to be in the *Divine Comedy*, a measure or standard whereby to contrast the different powers of the three great poets of our age. In Byron we see the austere plastic style and vivid expression,—the vengeance which Dante, embracing in the *Inferno*, the past, present, and future, exercises, in the name of universal judgment with prophetic force, but with personal hatred. In Shelley, as in the *Purgatorio*, we see the pains of the condemned in part picturesque, but the dark and fiery vapour giving place to the various play and greater pomp of the colouring; and in Wordsworth, *quel signor dell' altissimo canto*, the *Paradiso*, where shines the pure light, struck with whose refulgence the poet's mind seems at length to lay aside all reflection, and enjoy the intuition of perfect goodness, in the contemplation of love and the consummation of all things in happiness. Or to borrow an illustration from a sister art, we may compare them to the gigantic energy of Michael Angelo's figures, the fanciful incongruity of Raphael's Arabesques, and the calm yet sweetly animated serenity of Correggio's saints.

"Mr. Shelley's poetry," says a biographer, "is invested with a dazzling and subtle radiance which blinds the common observer with excess of light. Piercing beyond this, we discover that the characteristics of his poetical writings are an exceeding sympathy with the whole universe, material and intellectual—an ardent desire to benefit his species, and an impatience of the tyrannies and superstitions that hold them bound. In all his writings there is a wonderfully sustained sensibility, and a language lofty and fit for it. He has the art of using the stateliest words, and the most learned idioms, without incurring the charge of pedantry ; so that passages of more splendid and sonorous writing are not to be selected from any writer since the time of Milton ; and yet when he descends from his ideal worlds, and comes home to us in our humble bowers, and our yearnings after love and affection, he attunes the most natural feelings to a style so proportionate, and withal to a modulation so truly musical, that there is nothing to surpass it in the lyrics of Beaumont and Fletcher."

His is the poetry of intellect, not that of the lakers—his theme is the high one of intellectual nature and lofty feeling, not of waggoners or idiot children. Like Milton, he does not love to contemplate "clowns and vices," but the loftiest forms of excellence which his fancy can present. His morality has always reference to the virtues which he admires, and not to the vices of which he is either unconscious or ashamed. He looks upwards with passionate veneration, and seldom downwards with self-control. Instead of a simple and well-defined piece of music, his poetry is a brilliant fantasia, containing in itself the fragments of many melodies, but which, from its confusion, leaves on the ear no other remembrance of its modulations than the key-note. The imagery is chequered with unnatural lights and shadows, which, to the uninitiated, seem capriciously painted in a studio, without regard to the real nature of things; for to them, there is not apparent a system of "divine philosophy," like a sun reflecting order on his landscape. His poetry contains infinite sadness. It is the morbid expression of a soul "desperate," to use the beautiful words of Jeremy Taylor, "by a too quick sense of a constant infelicity." Like him who had returned from the valley of the dolorous abyss, the reader hears a voice of lamentation "wailing for the world's wrong," in accents wild and sweet, yet "incommunicably strange," but every thing to his sight is dark and cloudy when he attempts to penetrate beyond this obscure depth.

> "Che tuono accoglie d'infiniti guai,
> Oscura profonda era e nebulosa
> Tanto che, per ficcar lo viso a fondo,
> Io non vi discernea alcuna cosa."—*Inferno*.

The view of external objects suggests ideas and reflections, as if the poet's soul had awoke from slumber and saw, through a long vista, glimpses of a communion held with them in a distant past. It is like the first awaking of Adam, and the indistinct expression of his emotions. Nature is like a musical instrument, whose tones again are keys to higher strings in him; the morning light causing the statue of Memnon to sound. The shadow of some unseen power, as he himself has feigned of intellectual beauty, deriving much of its interest from its invisibility, floats, though unseen, among his verses; resembling every thing unreal and fantastic—the hues and harmonies of evening—the memory of music fled—

> "Or aught that for its grace may be,
> Dear, and yet dearer for its mystery."

And the only thing apparent, is a passionate regret that the power of one loving and enthusiastic individual was not proportioned to his will, nor his good reception with the world at all proportioned to his love. A misanthropy which so often has the effect of giving to strange and even revolting objects, (as for instance in the tragedy of the Cenci, a dark and horrible subject, fit only for the elder Crebillon,) the same fascination for his mind, as they possessed over that of the melancholy Florentine. From a sophistical analysis of the most natural ties and affections with which the mind, during those moments of despondency when its generous love feels the want of its powers to do good, or if enabled, is repulsed by an unfeeling world for its officiousness, will attempt to soothe itself into the dream of its own independence—he also frequently derives the expression of a ruthless philosophy; but when strong and immediate personal feelings have given a deeper tone and more pointed direction to his muse, as in the Elegy on the death of Adonais, a great and admirable change for the better is made on the perspicuity of his style. His metaphors become intelligible, his allusions forcible and applicable, his diction admirably precise, and that monotony of ideas which characterises his pathetic *Lyre of Love*: that flickering flame then bursts forth into the fire of an indignant prophet, now invoking vengeance on the head of him who pierced the innocent breast of his young friend—

"And scared the angel soul that was its earthly guest."

Now triumphing over the obscene ravens "clamorous o'er the dead."

"When like Apollo from his golden bow,
The Pythian of the age one arrow sped,
And smiled."

And finally dying away into those heartfelt convictions, with which, in every mythology, the virtuous human soul, succumbing to a dark and cruel fate, is regarded as a divine being, suffering in time, only to reveal the triumph of eternal glory, and the invisible beauty over frail earthly power; such elegies which lament, as it were, the mournful fate of all that is great and beautiful in individuals and nations, thus being sublime triumphal songs—the echoes of that beauty re-ascending to its native skies. How loftily is this proclaimed in the concluding stanza:

"The breath, whose might I have invoked in song,
Descends on me; my spirit's bark is driven
Far from the shore, far from the trembling throng,
Whose sails were never to the tempest given:—
The massy earth, and sphered skies are riven!
I am borne darkly, fearfully, afar;
Whilst burning through the inmost veil of Heaven,
The soul of Adonais, like a star,
Beacons from the abode where the Eternal are."

To such a mind as this life is but a disease of the spirit, a working incited by passion. Rest, the most desirable of all things—*Mors optima rerum*. His hypothesis of human perfectibility, and the progress from a sensual to an intellectual state in this life, which, contrary to all experience, is perpetually advocated—the consciousness of his own high aspirations teaching him "to fear himself and love all human kind"—and the attempt, though poetry should in reality be the original form of the soul, to make of idle verse, and idler prose, the framework of the universe, and to bind all possible existence in the visionary chain of intellectual beauty, both were indeed equally vain and enthusiastic.

> "To suffer woes which Hope thinks infinite—
> To forgive wrongs darker than death or night—
> To defy power, which seems omnipotent—
> To love and bear: to hope till hope creates
> From its own wreck the thing it contemplates,
> Neither to change, nor flatter, nor repent;
> This, like thy glory, Titan, is to be
> Good, great, and joyous, beautiful and free;
> This is alone life, joy, empire, and victory."

Alas for Adonais!

An ode, composed on the late French revolution, by an admirer of Shelley's poetry, has been pronounced, by competent judges, to be so fair an imitation of his solemn, stately diction, and exaggerated, yet significant allusions, that, although it breathes a spirit so democratic withal, that we suspect it is only in a journal like our own, whose staunch loyalty is so well known, that it would dare to be printed without fear of a visit from His Majesty's Attorney-General, we shall, nevertheless, present a few stanzas to the reader, without curtailing a single syllable :

" A sound as of a mighty angel singing,
  Or far off thunder, strikes my listening ear :
Now loud, now faint, by turns alternate ringing,
Whilst the loud echoes clearer and more clear,
O'er sky and cloud and each harmonious hill,
      Reverberate like harmony
      Of evening ; or melody
Of music heard in an autumnal sky,
Which dies yet leaves behind its sympathy to thrill.
Was it a voice ?—Perchance, while deeply musing
What heaven-oppressed mortality inherits—
The king-deluded world's ancestral ill,
Conjured before the sad o'erwearied spirit's
Faint organs, sounds as of the electric loosing
Of the Promethean adamantine chain.
Hark !—'tis the articulate voice—it comes again, again !

Mine eyes' clear orbits like the beaten flint,
Sparkle with fire ; a whirlwind wraps my soul ;
Dim visions float before me, and imprint
Their forms on earnest words, which as they roll,
The faltering tongue distinctly scarce pronounces—
      Last of the Labdacidæ,
      Listen to the prophecy,
Which, long begun, soon ends, alas ! in thee
Thought-winged liberty thy life denounces
And destiny with endless involution,
Fold: the high house of Œdipus—I see
The lesson shadowed in the past,—the fire
Dealt to another's pile, just retribution
Makes on its own creator back retire.
Invokest thou Celtic anarchs from the North ?
Call on Cimmerian wolves—What one shall dare come forth ?

Woe, woe!—the wrath of nations quick devours ;
As in the deep abyss of ocean sank

The countless host of the Egyptian powers,
So shall each Pharaoh banded 'gainst the Frank,
Fare in his impious war, and like thee perish.
      Tyrants, thrones, and priests all must
      Follow thee and come to dust.
Soon quail their high hearts in their impious trust,
Grovels their purple pride, when slaves that cherish
In their heart's heart freedom, the lamp of life,
Wait but her signal to leap forth, arrayed
In the resistless might of hate, and thrust
From its grey throne the Python, by whose aid
Power long hath poisoned all the springs of life.
Lamp of the earth! thy light all mists subdued;
Shout! for the world's young morn is, as a snake's, renewed.

All old things now are past away, and error
Flies like a cloud from the regenerate earth;
Immortal truth again holds up her mirror,
To wrongs engendered at the Hydra's birth.
And startled nations hail the wished commotion:
      When loud the voice divine,
      Let equal laws be thine,
And light and truth resounds from freedom's shrine,
Driving through the pale world a spirit of deep emotion.

      *   *   *   *   *

"Mr. Shelley when he died was in his thirtieth year. His figure was tall and slight, and his constitution consumptive. He was subject to violent spasmodic pains, which would sometimes force him to lie on the ground till they were over; but he had always a kind word to give to those about him when his pangs allowed him to speak. In his organization, as well as in other respects, he resembled the German poet, Schiller. Though well turned, his shoulders were bent a little, owing to premature thought and trouble. The same causes had touched his hair with grey; and though his habits of temperance and exercise gave him a remarkable degree of strength, it is not supposed that he could have lived many years. He used to say that he had lived three times as long as the calendar gave out, which he would prove between jest and earnest by some remarks on Time—

"That would have puzzled that stout Stagyrite.

Like the Stagyrite's, his voice was high and weak. His eyes were large and animated, with a dash of wildness in them; his face small, but well shaped, particularly the mouth and chin, the turn of which was very sensitive and graceful. His complexion was naturally fair and delicate, with a colour in the cheeks. He had brown hair, which, though tinged with grey, surmounted his face well, being in considerable quantity and tending to a curl."

"Non le connobbe il mondo mentre l'ebbe
Conobill' io ch' a pianger qui rimasi."

PETRARCA.

The important literary curiosity, which the liberality of the gentleman into whose hands it has fallen, enables us now to lay before the public, for the first time, in a complete state, was offered for publication by Mr. Shelley when quite a boy. It is certainly a wonderful attempt for a youth of seventeen, and there is in this early straining after the powerful and terrific, the germ of *Prometheus* and *Queen Mab*. In the latter poem, indeed, his old friend Ahasuerus is again introduced, with a quotation from the same German author, whom he here mentions, and also in the lyrical Drama of *Hellas*. The *Wandering Jew* has some weak passages, but many noble ones also. Its chief fault is the German *diablerie*, the fee, fa, fum of the fiends, which are here described with too much sameness, yet with all a schoolboy's notions of sublimity. He had not yet read Laplace. At school he is known to have been addicted to German and chemistry, and at the early age of fifteen wrote two novels, called the *Rosicrucian* and *Zastrozzi*, which we would give something to see now. There is a pretty, affecting passage at the end of the fourth canto, which we dare say bore reference to the cloud of family misfortune in which he was then enveloped.

> "Tis mournful when the deadliest hate
> Of friends, of fortune, and of fate
> Is levelled at one fated head."

The beginning of the first, and the whole of the third and last cantos are the finest. There is, perhaps, a poverty of rhymes and a want of variety in the mental imagery of the chief character, which is apt to tire. Poor Ahasuerus is so often "harrowed" and "parched," and "chilled" and "blasted," that he becomes like the sieve of Danaides, and we wonder at last how he comes to hold any impression at all; but, in conclusion, it is noble and elevated, and replete with pathos. The primitiæ of such a mind cannot be uninteresting to the lovers of his poetry, whatever they may seem to others.

NOTE.—It is worth mentioning that the following notice appeared on the cover of *Fraser's Magazine*, for July, 1831 :

"An obscure contemporary has accused us of announcing for publication, Shelley's poem without proper authority. We beg to assure him that we have the sanction of Mrs. Shelley.

"O. Y." [Oliver Yorke = W. Maginn.]

Mr. Tegetmeier first drew attention to this notice in the *Notebook* of the Shelley Society.

NOTES.

NOTES.

Page xxi. "*Preface.*"

It is rather remarkable that Medwin prints a passage from what, he informs us, was intended for the preface to *The Wandering Jew*, had it been published. He says (*Life of Shelley*, vol. i. p. 69) :—

"*The Rosicrucian*[1] was suggested by *St. Leon*, which Shelley wonderfully admired. He read it till he believed that there was truth in Alchymy, and the *Elixir Vitæ*, which indeed entered into the plot of the *Wandering Jew*, of which I possess a preface by him, intended for the poem, had it been published. He says :—'The opinion that gold can be made, passed from the Arabs to the Greeks, and from the Greeks to the rest of Europe; those who professed it, gradually assumed the form of a sect, under the name of Alchymists. These Alchymists laid it down as a first principle, that all metals are composed of the same materials, or that the substances at least that form gold, exist in all metals, contaminated indeed by various impurities, but capable of being brought to a perfect state, by purification; and hence that considerable quantities of gold might be extracted from them. The generality of this belief in the eastern provinces of the Roman Empire, is proved by a remarkable edict of Diocletian, quoted by Gibbon from the authority of two ancient historians, &c.'"

[1] *St. Irvyne; or the Rosicrucian.*

If Shelley ever wrote the Preface from which Medwin quotes, it was probably intended for some other work, for there is no reference in *The Wandering Jew* to the *Elixir Vitæ*, and it is very unlikely that he wrote two Prefaces to the poem.

Page xxix. "*The crucifixion scene altogether a plagiarism from a volume of Cambridge Prize Poems.*"

The following extracts from Thomas Zouch's poem of "The Crucifixion," (which is a capital specimen of the Brummagem Miltonic sublime) are the only ones that bear any resemblance to the passage relating to the same subject in *The Wandering Jew*.

"Memory bids the scene,
Th' important scene, arise, when dread dismay
Alarm'd the nations. Melt, thou heart of brass:
Death triumph'd o'er its victor. Wild amaze
Seiz'd all the host of heaven, moaning their God
In agony transfixt, his every sense
A window to affliction: sorrow fill'd
Their tide of tragic woe, and chang'd the note
From fervent rapture to the gloomy strain
Of deepest lamentation."

"Ye young, ye gay,
Listen with patient ear the strains of truth:
Ye who in dissipation waste your days,
From pleasure's giddy train O steal an hour,
With sage reflection, nor disdain to gaze
The solemn scene on Calv'ry's guilty mount,
Where frighted nature shakes her trembling frame,
And shudders at the complicated crime
Of deicide.—The thorn-encircled head
All pale and languid on the bleeding cross,
The nail-empierced hand, the mangled feet,

The perforated side, the heaving sigh
Of gushing anguish, the deep groan of death,
The day of darkness, terror and distress :
Ah ! shall not these awake one serious thought ! "

" See Israel's humble King, mild as the lamb
Beneath the murdering knife, amidst the sneer,
The taunt of mad reproach, led to the cross,
To shame and bitter death. Him late they rais'd
To fame's bright summit, when they sung his name
With loud hosannas, or with silent ardor
Dwelt on his tongue, list'ning the happy lore
Of evangelic joy. Ye ruffian tribe,
Ah ! check the ruthless rage, that drowns the voice,
The faithful voice of reason, to your God
Prefers sedition's son, whom foul with crimes,
Ripe vengeance waits, and awful justice calls."

Page xxvi. *"the vision in the third canto taken from Lewis's 'Monk.'"*

The vision referred to seems to be that of Don Lorenzo, in the first chapter of "The Monk :" but, as I have said, there is no great likeness between the two visions. The following passage is the only one which bears any positive resemblance to Shelley's verses :—

" At the same moment the roof of the cathedral opened ; harmonious voices pealed along the vaults ; and the glory into which Antonia was received, was composed of rays of such dazzling brightness, that Lorenzo was unable to sustain the gaze. His sight failed, and he sank upon the ground."

As few persons nowadays have the desire or opportunity to read "The Monk," it seems worth while to give a short account of the manner in which the Wandering Jew is introduced into it, in order to show how much Shelley was indebted to that medley of pruriency and of melodramatic horrors. It is in the fourth chapter, which relates the story of Don Raymond and the bleeding nun, that the Jew appears. Don Raymond is lying wounded at a country inn, where he is tormented each night by the appearance of the apparition of the bleeding nun. He is reduced by its visitations to the last degree of weakness and distress, and his only solace is in the company of his attendant, a youth named Theodore. The reader will now be in a position to understand the following extract from the novel, it being premised that Don Raymond himself relates the story :—

"One evening I was lying upon my sopha, plunged in reflections very far from agreeable: Theodore amused himself by observing from the window a battle between two postilions, who were quarrelling in the inn-yard.

"Ha! ha!" cried he suddenly, "yonder is the Great Mogul."

"Who?" said I.

"Only a man who made me a strange speech at Munich."

"What was the purport of it?"

"Now you put me in mind of it, Segnor, it was a kind of message to you, but truly it was not worth delivering. I believe the fellow to be mad, for my part. When I came to Munich in search of you, I found him living at "the King of the Romans," and the host gave me an odd account of him. By his accent he is supposed to be a foreigner, but of what country nobody can tell. He seemed to have no acquaintance in the town, spoke very seldom, and never was seen to smile. He had neither servants nor baggage; but his purse seemed well furnished, and he did much good in the town. Some supposed him to be an Arabian astrologer, others to be a travelling mountebank, and many declared that he was Doctor Faustus, whom the devil had sent back to Germany. The landlord, however, told me, that he had the best reasons to believe him to be the Great Mogul incognito."

"But the strange speech, Theodore—"

"True, I had almost forgotten the speech: indeed, for that matter, it would not have been a great loss if I had forgotten it altogether. You are to know, Segnor, that while I was enquiring about you of the landlord, this stranger passed by. He stopped, and looked at me earnestly—'Youth,' said he, in a solemn voice, 'he whom you seek, has found that which he would fain lose. My hand alone can dry up the blood. Bid your master wish for me when the clock strikes one.'"

"How?" cried I, starting from my sopha. [The words which Theodore had repeated, seemed to imply the stranger's knowledge of my secret] "Fly to him, my boy! Entreat him to grant me one moment's conversation."

Theodore was surprised at the vivacity of my manner; however, he asked no questions, but hastened to obey me. I waited his return impatiently. But a short space of time had elapsed, when he again appeared, and ushered the expected guest into my chamber. He was a man of majestic presence; his countenance was strongly marked, and his eyes were large, black, and sparkling: yet there was a something in his look, which, the moment that I saw him, inspired me with a secret awe, not to say horror. He was dressed plainly, his hair was unpowdered, and a band of black velvet which encircled his forehead, spread over his features an additional gloom. His countenance wore the marks of profound melancholy, his step was slow, and his manner grave, stately, and solemn.

He saluted me with politeness; and having replied to the usual compliments of introduction, he motioned to Theodore to quit the chamber. The page instantly withdrew.

"I know your business," said he, without giving me time to speak. "I have the power of releasing you from your nightly visitor; but this cannot be done before Sunday. On the hour when the Sabbath morning breaks, spirits of darkness have least influence over mortals. After Saturday the nun shall visit you no more."

"May I not enquire," said I, "by what means you are in possession of a secret, which I have carefully concealed from the knowledge of every one?"

"How can I be ignorant of your distresses, when their cause at this moment stands beside you?"

I started. The stranger continued.

"Though to you only visible for one hour in the twenty-four, neither day nor night does she ever quit you; nor will she ever quit you till you have granted her request."

"And what is that request?"

"That she must herself explain: it lies not in my knowledge. Wait with patience for the night of Saturday: all shall be then cleared up."

I dared not press him further. He soon after changed the conversation, and talked of various matters. He named people who had ceased to exist for many centuries, and yet with whom he appeared to have been personally acquainted. I could not mention a country, however distant, which he had not visited, nor could I sufficiently admire the extent and variety of his information. I remarked to him, that having travelled, seen and known so much, must have given him infinite pleasure. He shook his head mournfully.

"No one," he replied, "is adequate to comprehending the misery of my lot! Fate obliges me to be constantly in movement; I am not permitted to pass more than a fortnight in the same place. I have no friend in the world, and from the restlessness of my destiny, I never can acquire one. Fain would I lay down my miserable life, for I envy those who enjoy the quiet of the grave: but death eludes me, and flies from my embrace. In vain do I throw myself in the way of danger. I plunge into the ocean; the waves throw me back with abhorrence upon the shore: I rush into fire: the flames recoil at my approach: I oppose myself to the fury of banditti; their swords become blunted, and break against my breast. The hungry tiger shudders at my approach, and the alligator flies from a monster more horrible than itself. God has set his seal upon me, and all his creatures respect this fatal mark."

He put his hand to the velvet, which was bound round his forehead. There was in his eyes an expression of fury, despair, and malevolence, that struck horror to my very soul. An involuntary convulsion made me shudder. The stranger perceived it.

"Such is the curse imposed on me," he continued: "I am doomed to inspire all who look on me with terror and detestation. You already feel the influence of the charm, and with every succeeding moment will feel it more. I will not add to your sufferings by my presence. Farewell, till Saturday. As soon as the clock strikes twelve, expect me at your chamber."

Having said this he departed, leaving me in astonishment at the mysterious turn of his manner and conversation. His assurances that I should soon be relieved from the apparition's visits, produced a good effect upon my constitution. Theodore, who I rather treated as an adopted child than a domestic, was surprised at his return to observe the amendment in my looks. —He congratulated me on this symptom of returning health, and declared himself delighted at my having received so much benefit from my conference with the Great Mogul. Upon inquiry I found that the stranger had already passed eight days in Ratisbon. According to his own account, therefore, he was only to remain there six days longer. Saturday was still at the distance of three. Oh! with what impatience did I expect its arrival! In the interim, the bleeding nun continued her nocturnal visits; but hoping soon to be released from them altogether, the effects which they produced on me became less violent than before.

The wished-for night arrived. To avoid creating suspicion, I retired to bed at my usual hour. But as soon as my attendants had left me, I dressed myself again, and prepared for the stranger's reception. He entered my room upon the turn of midnight. A small chest was in his hand, which he placed near the stove. He saluted me without speaking; I returned the compliment, observing an equal silence. He then opened the chest. The first thing which he produced was a small wooden crucifix; he sunk upon his knees, gazed upon it mournfully, and cast his eyes towards heaven. He seemed to be praying devoutly. At length he bowed his head respectfully, kissed the crucifix thrice, and quitted his kneeling posture. He next drew from the chest a covered goblet: with the liquor which it contained, and which appeared to be blood, he sprinkled the floor; and then dipping in it one end of the crucifix, he described a circle in the middle of the room. Round about this he placed various reliques, skulls, thigh-bones, &c. I observed, that he disposed them all in the forms of crosses. Lastly, he took out a large Bible, and beckoned me to follow him into the circle. I obeyed.

"Be cautious not to utter a syllable!" whispered the stranger: "step not out of the circle, and as you love yourself, dare not to look upon my face!"

Holding the crucifix in one hand, the Bible in the other, he seemed to read with profound attention. The clock struck one; as usual I heard the spectre's steps upon the staircase: but I was not seized with the accustomed shivering. I waited her approach with confidence. She entered the room, drew near the circle, and stopped.—The stranger muttered some words, to me unintelligible. Then raising his head from the book, and extending the crucifix towards the ghost, he pronounced, in a voice distinct and solemn,

"Beatrice! Beatrice! Beatrice!"

"What wouldst thou?" replied the apparition in a hollow faltering tone.

"What disturbs thy sleep? Why dost thou afflict and torture this youth? How can rest be restored to thy inquiet spirit?"

"I dare not tell! I must not tell! Fain would I repose in my grave, but stern commands force me to prolong my punishment."

"Knowest thou this blood? Knowest thou in whose veins it flowed? Beatrice! Beatrice! In his name, I charge thee to answer me."

"I dare not disobey my taskers."

"Darest thou disobey me?"

He spoke in a commanding tone, and drew the sable band from his forehead.—In spite of his injunction to the contrary, curiosity would not suffer me to keep my eyes off his face: I raised them, and beheld a burning cross impressed upon his brow. For the horror with which this object inspired me I cannot account, but I never felt its equal. My senses left me for some moments: a mysterious dread overcame my courage; and had not the exorciser caught my hand, I should have fallen out of the circle.

When I recovered myself, I perceived that the burning cross had produced an effect no less violent upon the spectre. Her countenance expressed reverence and horror, and her visionary limbs were shaken by fear.

"Yes!" she said at length, "I tremble at that mark! I respect it! I obey you! Know then, that my bones lie still unburied: they rot in the obscurity of Lindenberg-hole. None but this youth has the right of consigning them to the grave.——His own lips have made over to me his body and his soul: never will I give back his promise; never shall he know a night devoid of terror, unless he engages to collect my mouldering bones, and deposit them in the family vault of his Andalusian castle. Then let thirty masses be said for the repose of my spirit, and I trouble this world no more. Now let me depart. Those flames are scorching."

He let the hand drop slowly which held the crucifix, and which till then he had pointed towards her. The apparition bowed her head, and her form melted into air. The exorciser led me out of the circle. He replaced the Bible, &c. in the chest, and then addressed himself to me, who stood near him speechless from astonishment.

"Don Raymond, you have heard the conditions on which

repose is promised you. Be it your business to fulfil them to the letter. For me, nothing more remains than to clear up the darkness still spread over the spectre's history, and inform you, that when living, Beatrice bore the name of las Cisternas. She was the great-aunt of your grandfather. In quality of your relation, her ashes demand respect from you, though the enormity of her crimes must excite your abhorrence. The nature of those crimes no one is more capable of explaining to you than myself. I was personally acquainted with the holy man who proscribed her nocturnal riots in the castle of Lindenberg, and I hold this narrative from his own lips."

It is unnecessary to trouble the reader with the account of the crimes which entailed such a severe punishment upon Beatrice de las Cisternas. The Wandering Jew thus concludes his relation of them :—

"She was doomed to suffer during the space of a century. That period is past. Nothing now remains but to consign to the grave the ashes of Beatrice. I have been the means of releasing you from your visionary tormentor ; and amidst all the sorrows which oppress me, to think that I have been of use to you, is some consolation. Youth, farewell! May the ghost of your relation enjoy that rest in the tomb, which the Almighty's vengeance has denied to me for ever!"

Here the stranger prepared to quit the apartment.

"Stay yet one moment!" said I; "you have satisfied my curiosity with regard to the spectre, but you leave me a prey to yet greater respecting yourself. Deign to inform me to whom I am under such real obligations. You mention circumstances long past, and persons long dead : you were personally acquainted with the exorciser, who, by your own account, has been deceased near a century. How am I to account for this ? What means that burning cross upon your forehead, and why did the sight of it strike such horror to my soul?"

On these points he for some time refused to satisfy me.

At length, overcome by my entreaties, he consented to clear up the whole, on condition that I would defer his explanation till the next day. With this request I was obliged to comply, and he left me. In the morning my first care was to inquire after the mysterious stranger. Conceive my disappointment, when informed that he had already quitted Ratisbon. I despatched messengers in pursuit of him, but in vain. No traces of the fugitive were discovered. Since that moment I never have heard any more of him, and 'tis most probable that I never shall."

[Lorenzo here interrupted his friend's narrative:

"How?" said he, "you have never discovered who he was, or even formed a guess?"

"Pardon me," replied the marquis: "when I related this adventure to my uncle, the cardinal duke, he told me, that he had no doubt of this singular man's being the celebrated character known universally by the name of *the wandering Jew*. His not being permitted to pass more than fourteen days on the same spot, the burning cross impressed upon his forehead, the effect which it produced upon the beholders, and many other circumstances, gave this supposition the colour of truth. The cardinal is fully persuaded of it; and for my own part I am inclined to adopt the only solution which offers itself to this riddle." I return to the narrative from which I have digressed.]"

Page xxx. "*In short the conclusions I have come to, &c.*"

The evidence of Mrs. Shelley may be quoted as additional proof of Shelley's authorship of the poem. In her "Note on *Queen Mab*," (Poetical Works of Shelley, 1839, vol. i. p. 102), she says:—

"He wrote also a poem on the subject of Ahasuerus— being led to it by a German fragment he picked up, dirty and torn, in Lincoln's Inn Fields. This fell afterwards into other hands—and was considerably altered before it was printed."

As to the statement that the poem was considerably altered before its appearance in print, I do not think we need infer that any material alterations were made in it, but only that passages may have been abridged or omitted at the Editor's discretion. It is to be remembered that the poem was published with Mrs. Shelley's consent in *Fraser's Magazine*, and it can hardly be thought that her permission would have been given if she had not believed in her husband's authorship of it. It may be thought perhaps that her evidence does not go for much, as the poem was written long before she became acquainted with Shelley. It is likely, however, that he, at some time, would tell her of his early poem ; and, as Medwin was in 1821 an inmate of their household, nothing is more likely than that *The Wandering Jew* would become the subject of conversation between them. That Mrs. Shelley says nothing of Medwin in connection with the poem (although he had already advanced his claim to it) goes a good way toward proving that it was Shelley's.

Page 2. "*So soft the clime, so balm the air.*"

It is perhaps worth mentioning that, in the selections printed in the *Literary Journal*, the lines are indented throughout, which is not the case in *Fraser*. This may help to show that the MS. used by the *Literary Journal* was a more carefully prepared and finished one than the *Fraser* version. As the present edition is taken mainly from the *Fraser* copy, it seemed proper, for the sake of uniformity, to print it throughout in the same manner as in that magazine. As an example, I quote a few lines as printed in the *Edinburgh Journal* :—

"So soft the clime, so balm the air,
　So pure and genial were the skies,
　In sooth 'twas almost Paradise,—
　For ne'er did the sun's splendour close
　On such a picture of repose ;"—

Page 6. "*Melting, kindling, raising, firing,
Delighting now, and now inspiring.*"

This seems to be a reminiscence of Pope's

"Trembling, hoping, ling'ring, flying,
Oh the pain, the bliss of dying!"

Pope indeed borrowed from Flatman, who has

" Fainting, gasping, trembling, crying,
Panting, groaning, speechless, dying,"

but it is hardly likely that Shelley was acquainted with Flatman's verses.

Page 12. "' *And, ah!*' *cried he,* '*be this the band.*'"

There is a passage resembling this in *St. Irvyne*:—

" Never, never shall it end!" enthusiastically exclaimed Wolfstein. "Never!—What can break the bond joined by congeniality of sentiment, cemented by a union of soul which must endure till the intellectual particles which compose it become annihilated? Oh! never shall it end; for when, convulsed by nature's latest ruin, sinks the fabric of this perishable globe; when the earth is dissolved away, and the face of heaven is rolled from before our eyes like a scroll; then will we seek each other, and in eternal, indivisible, although immaterial union, shall we exist to all eternity."

There is also a similar passage in *Zastrozzi*:—

"'Shall I then call him mine for ever?' mentally inquired Matilda; 'will the passion which now consumes me, possess my soul to all eternity? Ah! well I know it will; and when emancipated from this terrestrial form, my soul departs; still its fervent energies unrepressed, will remain; and in the union of soul to soul, it will taste celestial transports.'"

It is very interesting to compare with these fictitious sentiments, the ones which occurred to Shelley himself, when he thought he was in imminent danger of being drowned together with his beloved Mary. Crossing the Channel with her after the elopement, a storm came on :—

"Mary did not know our danger; she was resting between my knees, that were unable to support her; she did not speak or look, but I felt that she was there. I had time in that moment to reflect and even to reason upon death; it was rather a thing of discomfort and of disappointment than horror to me. We should never be separated, but in death we might not know and feel our union as now. I hope, but my hopes are not unmixed with fear for what will befall this inestimable spirit when we appear to die."

Dowden's *Life of Shelley*, vol. i. p. 442.

Page 12.   "*Rosa, wilt thou then be mine?*
              Ever fairest, I am thine!"

This seems to be a reminiscence of a passage in *The Monk* :—

"'Agnes!' said I, while I pressed her to my bosom,
  'Agnes! Agnes! thou art mine!
  Agnes! Agnes! I am thine!
  In my veins while blood shall roll,
  Thou art mine!
  I am thine!
  Thine my body! thine my soul!'"

Page 21.   "*Why then unbidden gush'd the tear?*"

The passage beginning thus is used, with some omissions and alterations, as a motto to the eighth chapter of *St. Irvyne* :—

"—Why then unbidden gush'd the tear?
 .   .   .   .   .   .
 Then would cold shudderings seize his brain,
   As gasping he labour'd for breath;
 The strange gaze of his meteor eye,

> Which, frenzied, and rolling dreadfully,
>   Glar'd with hideous gleam,
> Would chill like the spectre gaze of Death,
>   As, conjur'd by feverish dream,
> He seems o'er the sick man's couch to stand,
> And shakes the fell lance in his skeleton hand."

Page 22.   " *The ministering angel hung,*
   And wiped the drops of agony."

Evidently a reminiscence of Scott's eulogium of woman :—

> " When pain and anguish wring the brow
> A ministering angel thou ! "

It seems likely that Scott, when he wrote these lines, remembered (perhaps unconsciously) the words of *Laertes* :—

> " I tell thee, churlish priest,
> A minist'ring angel shall my sister be,
> When thou liest howling."

Page 31.   "*And painted Hell upon the skies.*"

This image is repeated in a slightly altered form :—

" And the lightnings of God painting hell on the air." (p. 40)

Page 33.   "*I cursed the mother who gave me birth.*"

This line occurs again :—

"And cursed the mother who gave me birth." (p. 40)

Page 36.   " *But the wild surge swept my corpse ashore,*
   I was not with the dead ! "

This is an excellent " bull," and almost worthy of Sir Boyle Roche himself.   A similar one will be found on page 30 :—

"Still life prolonging after life was fled."

In the *Literary Journal* version the first of these blunders does not appear, a fact which helps to prove that it was the more finished rendering of the two.

Page 36. *"I cast myself from the overhanging summit of the gigantic Teneriffe."*

It is rather remarkable that this passage is different from the one of similar purport which Shelley quotes in *Queen Mab*, although both are said to be by a German author. As regards the present passage, it is not known, I believe, to what German author it is to be attributed; but the one in *Queen Mab* has been traced to a poem by Schubart, "the unlucky." It is, however, by no means a literal translation, but rather a free rendering, with additions. I learn from a MS. note in a copy of Shelley's Works which belonged to the late James Thomson that this poem of Schubart's was translated by the late Clarence Mangan, who inserted it in one of his *German Anthology* papers in the *Dublin University Magazine*.

Page 37. "*The elements respect their Maker's seal.*"

The passage beginning thus is quoted, with some variations, as a motto to the tenth chapter of *St. Irvyne*:—

> "The elements respect their Maker's seal!
> Still like the scathed pine-tree's height,
> Braving the tempests of the night,
> Have I scap'd the bickering flame,
> Like the scath'd pine, which a monument stands
> Of faded grandeur, which the brands
>   Of the tempest-shaken air
> Have riven on the desolate heath;
> Yet it stands majestic even in death,
>   And rears its wild form there."

In *Queen Mab* Shelley uses the same simile, only substituting *oak* for *pine*. "Thus," says Ahasuerus:—

"Thus have I stood,—through a wild waste of years
Struggling with whirlwinds of mad agony,
Yet peaceful, and serene, and self-enshrined,
Mocking my powerless tyrant's horrible curse
With stubborn and unalterable will,
Even as a giant oak, which heaven's fierce flame
Had scathèd in the wilderness, to stand
A monument of fadeless ruin there;
Yet peacefully and movelessly it braves
The midnight conflict of the wintry storm,
  As in the sun-light's calm it spread
  Its worn and withered arms on high
To meet the quiet of a summer's noon."

The simile is taken from the passage from a German author, which is quoted on page 36.

Page 47. "*Ah! why does man whom God has sent.*"
This passage is so singular—not in itself, but as coming from Shelley—that it is worth considering with particular attention. It may be observed first, that there is no apparent reason for its introduction, since it has no connection either with what has preceded or with what follows it. I infer therefore that it was written independently, and inserted in *The Wandering Jew* rather because the author did not like to lose it, than because it was in any way appropriate. Next, it is to be noted that in the concluding lines, beginning:—

"What then is man, how few his days,"

the sentiment is inconsistent with that of the opening verses. This makes me think that Shelley's original design was to write a poem in which the question as to man's relations with the Deity should be discussed between two speakers. If I am right in this conjecture the lines from the beginning of the Canto down to

"In misery live, despairing die,"

belong to the advocate of orthodox opinions; while the following lines represent the pleading of the unorthodox speaker. I do not, however, assert this very positively, for it may be that the passage as it stands simply represents the wavering and uncertain state of the author's mind at the time when the poem was written. It might be thought that this passage was one of those contributed by Medwin, but I do not think this can have been the case. There is one expression in it which occurs also in the *Alastor* volume, and which goes far towards showing that Shelley must have been the writer. Compare—

"The glory of the moon by night,"

with

"The glory of the moon is dead,"

which occurs in the poem beginning

"O! there are spirits of the air."

Page 54. "*Bursting through clouds of sulphurous smoke,*
As on a witch's form it broke:"

Medwin states that this description of the Witch was versified from a passage in a novel called *Nightmare*, which he and Shelley wrote in conjunction.

Page 60. "*Satan a shapeless, hideous beast—*
In all his horrors stood confest!"

This description of the summoning and the appearance of Satan seems to be borrowed, or at least derived, from a similar passage in *The Monk*. Ambrosio, having been sentenced to death, is awaiting in his prison the time of his execution. He uses a charm which causes Satan to appear :—

"A loud burst of thunder was heard, the prison shook to its very foundation, a blaze of lightning flashed through the cell, and in the next moment, borne upon sulphurous whirlwinds, Lucifer stood before him a second time. But he came not as when at Matilda's summons he borrowed the seraph's form to deceive Ambrosio. He appeared in all that ugliness, which since his fall from Heaven had been his portion. His blasted limbs still bore marks of the Almighty's thunder. A swarthy darkness spread itself over his gigantic form : his hands and feet were armed with long talons. Fury glared in his eyes, which might have struck the bravest heart with terror."

There is more of this stuff, but probably the reader will think I have quoted enough of it. Lewis might have been excused for writing it on the plea that he was very young when he did so, but for the fact that he continued to write such rubbish as long as he lived.

Page 71. "*Introductory Article.*"

One would like to know by whom this article, so appreciative of Shelley's genius at a time when appreciation was the exception and not the rule, was written. Medwin was inclined to think that Carlyle (he spells his name "Carlisle") was the author, but this was a very unlucky guess. Other names that suggest themselves are those of Mrs. Shelley, Leigh Hunt, T. L. Peacock, Horace Smith, and Thomas Wade, but all of them are more or less unlikely.

Page 72. "*The able and willing author.*"

This refers to William Hazlitt, who reviewed Shelley's *Posthumous Poems* in the *Edinburgh Review*. The "opposite

Aristarchus" doubtless refers to the critic of the *Quarterly Review*.

Page 75. "*Thus there is, blindly woven through the web of our being.*"

> " —that sustaining love
> Which through the web of being blindly wove
> By man and beast and earth and air and sea,
> Burns bright or dim, as each are mirrors of
> The fire for which all thirst ;—"
>
> *Adonais.*

Page 80. "*There is, indeed, a woe too deep for tears.*"

> " It is a woe too 'deep for tears,' when all
> Is reft at once, when some surpassing Spirit,
> Whose light adorned the world around it, leaves
> Those who remain behind, not sobs or groans,
> The passionate tumult of a clinging hope ;
> But pale despair and cold tranquillity,
> Nature's vast frame, the web of human things,
> Birth and the grave, that are not as they were."
>
> *Alastor.*

Page 81. "*Which does not disdain to regard,*" &c.

There seems to be some error in this sentence which renders its meaning obscure, if not unintelligible. I suspect it should read, " which disdains to regard even the greatest of heroes, of catastrophes, and of geniuses," &c.

Page 83. "' *Mr. Shelley's poetry,*' *says a biographer.*"

This passage is quoted from Leigh Hunt's *Lord Byron and Some of his Contemporaries.*

Page 89. "*Shout! for the world's young morn is, as a snake's, renewed.*"

> "The world's great age begins anew,
> The golden years return,
> The earth doth like a snake renew
> Her winter weeds outworn."
>
> *Hellas.*

Page 89. "*Mr. Shelley when he died.*"

This also is a quotation from Hunt's *Lord Byron and Some of his Contemporaries.*

Page 87. "*He used to say that he had lived.*"

See one of the notes to *Queen Mab*, where this idea is dwelt upon at length. One sentence in this note was an unconscious prediction. "Thus, the life of a man of virtue and talent *who should die in his thirtieth year*, is, with regard to his own feelings longer than that of a priest-ridden slave, who dreams out a century of dulness." A few days before his death, he said to Mrs. Hunt, "If I die to-morrow, I have lived to be older than my father; I am ninety years of age."

Page 91. "'*Tis mournful when the deadliest hate.*"

It is very singular that these interesting lines do not appear in the poem, as published in *Fraser*. I can only suppose that they were cut out in the process of condensation which the poem seems to have undergone before it was printed. This is very unlucky, for they arouse curiosity, and lead one to think that the passage from which they are taken must have been the best in the poem, because a direct transcript from the author's experience, and not a mere reflex of his reading.

RICHARD CLAY AND SONS,
LONDON AND BUNGAY.

February 10th, 1887.]

You are invited to join

THE SHELLEY SOCIETY.

THE Yearly Subscription (which constitutes Membership) is One Guinea, due every first of January, beginning January 1st, 1886, and should be paid to either the *Honorary Secretary*,

 JAMES STANLEY LITTLE, Esq.,
  76, Clarendon Road, Holland Park, W.,
or to the *Chairman of Committee*,
 WILLIAM MICHAEL ROSSETTI, Esq.,
  5, Endsleigh Gardens, Euston Road, London, N.W.

(The American Subscription is $5.25, and may be paid as above, or to any Local Hon. Sec. in the United States: see p. 2.)

This Subscription entitles a Member to one copy of all the Publications of the Society during the current year (with a second copy of the *Note-Book*[1]); to attend, and introduce a friend to, all the Society's Meetings; and to admission to the Society's performances of Shelley's *Cenci* or *Hellas*, or (if the Society's funds allow of it) to both.

The following seven books will form the first issue of the Society's Publications for 1887. A list of those further proposed will be found on pages 21 and 22.

1. *The Wandering Jew*, a Poem by Percy Bysshe Shelley. Edited by Bertram Dobell. [*Issued.*
2. *The Shelley Primer*, by H. S. Salt, M.A. [*Issued.*
3. The Pianoforte Score of Dr. W. C. Selle's Choruses and Recitations, composed for the Society's performance of Shelley's *Hellas* in November, 1886. [*Issued.*
4. *An Address to the Irish People*, by Percy Bysshe Shelley. A Type-facsimile Reprint on Hand-made Paper. Edited by Thomas J. Wise.
  [*Ready immediately.*
5. *The Necessity of Atheism*, by Percy Bysshe Shelley. A Type-facsimile Reprint on Hand-made Paper. Edited by Thomas J. Wise.
  [*Ready immediately.*
6. *The Masque of Anarchy*, by Percy Bysshe Shelley. A Type-facsimile Reprint on Hand-made paper. Edited by Thomas J. Wise.
  [*Ready immediately.*
7. *Epipsychidion*, by Percy Bysshe Shelley. A Type-facsimile Reprint upon Hand-made Paper, with an Introduction by the Rev. Stopford A. Brooke, M.A., and a Note by Algernon Charles Swinburne. Edited by Robert A. Potts. [*Ready immediately.*

[1] That is, *one* copy in separate numbers, and a *second* copy as a complete Part.

COMMITTEE.

William E. A. Axon.
Miss Mathilde Blind.
Rev. Stopford A. Brooke, M.A.
Bertram Dobell.
F. S. Ellis.
Alfred Forman.
H. Buxton Forman.
Fredk. J. Furnivall, M.A., Ph.D.
    (*Treasurer*.)
Charles Gordon Hall.
Rev. W. A. Harrison, M.A.
Prof. A. S. Napier, M.A., Ph.D.

Robert Alfred Potts.
William Michael Rossetti.
    (*Chairman*.)
H. S. Salt.
Gabriel Sarrazin.
William Bell Scott.
Henry Sweet, M.A., Ph.D.
W. B. Tegetmeier.
John Todhunter, M.D
A. W. Verrall, M.A.
Hermann Vezin.
Thomas J. Wise.

Hon. Sec., James Stanley Little, 76, Clarendon Road, Holland Park, London, W.

Bank: London and County, Holborn Branch, 324, High Holborn, W.C.
Publishers: Reeves and Turner, 196, Strand, London, W.C.
Agents: Charles Hutt, Clement's Inn Gateway, Strand, London, W.C.
    Bertram Dobell, 66, Queen's Crescent, Haverstock Hill, London, N.W.
Printers: R. Clay and Sons, Bread Street Hill, London, E.C.

LOCAL HONORARY SECRETARIES.

Auckland, New Zealand: Prof. H. M. Posnett, University.
Birmingham: W. Kineton Parkes, Summerfield Crescent, Edgbaston.
Cambridge: H. C. Marillier, Peterhouse.
Cambridge, Massachusetts, U.S.A.: Prof. J. M. Peirce, 4, Kirkland Place.
Hackney: E. Berdoe, Tynemouth House, Victoria Park Gate.
Manchester: T. C. Abbott, Eastlegh, Queen's Road, Bowdon.
Melbourne, Victoria: Frank Scrivenor, 28, Market Square, Collins Street West.
Newcastle-on-Tyne: Fred. Grahame Aylward, 51, Westmoreland Road, Newcastle-on-Tyne.
New York (Northern): Addison Child, Childwold.
New York: Charles W. Frederickson, 741, Lexington Avenue.
Oxford:
Reading: J. J. Rossiter, 12, Abbot's Walk, Forbury Gardens.
Uxbridge: Alfred Fountain, Highfield, Hillingdon.

    The Committee wish to see a large number of Branch Shelley Societies and Local Shelley Reading Clubs established, out of London, and in its suburbs. They will be glad to appoint as *Local Honorary Secretaries* such persons as will undertake to do what they can to promote the study of Shelley in their different localities.

The Society's Meetings and Papers during its Second Session, 1887, will be at University College, Gower Street, at 8 P.M. on Wednesdays.

Jan. 26. First Annual General Meeting.
Feb. 9. "On *The Triumph of Life*," by JOHN TODHUNTER, M.D.
March 9. "Miss Alma Murray as 'Beatrice Cenci,'" by B. L. MOSELY, LL.B
April 13. "On *The Revolt of Islam*," by ALEX. GALT ROSS, B.A.
May 11. Concert of Shelley Songs.
June 8. "Lord Beaconsfield and Shelley," by Dr. R. GARNETT.
Oct. 12.
Nov. 9.
Dec. 14.

A Lecture on "The Poetical and Dramatic Treatment of Shelley's *Prometheus Unbound*" will be delivered by Mr. W. M. ROSSETTI during the Session 1887-8. The date will be duly announced. Miss BLIND is also preparing for the same session a Lecture on "Shelley's Women."

Offers of Papers are desired, and should be made to the Chairman of Committee, Mr. W. M. ROSSETTI, or the Honorary Secretary, Mr. JAMES STANLEY LITTLE.

The following Papers were read before the Society during its First Session, 1886 :—

March 10. Inaugural Address on "Shelley," by the Rev. STOPFORD A. BROOKE, M.A.
April 14. "On the Vicissitudes of *Queen Mab*," by H. BUXTON FORMAN.
May 12. "On the Religion of Shelley," by F. J. MAYNARD, of St. John's College, Oxford.[1]
Nov. 10. "Shelley's View of Nature contrasted with Darwin's," by Miss MATHILDE BLIND.
Dec. 15. "A Study of *Prometheus Unbound*," by WILLIAM MICHAEL ROSSETTI.[2]

The Committee hope that some Members will give the Society other Facsimile Reprints, in addition to those already promised. An estimate of the cost of reproducing all the original editions of Shelley's different works will be given shortly in the Society's *Note-Book*, or may be had at once upon application. Two or more friends may well join in the gift of a book.

Shelley's Autobiography, by Mr. W. M. Rossetti—(see p. 10, Series IV., No. 7)—has long been prepared, and can be revised, completed, and sent to press, as soon as the Society has money enough to print it. This could be in 1888 if the Society's membership reaches the number of 500 in 1887.

[1] This was substituted at a few minutes' notice for the Paper previously promised for the evening, viz., "On the Primitiveness of Shelley's View of Nature, its Parallelism with that of the Vedas, and its contrast with that of Shakspere and other Poets," by HY. SWEET, M.A.
[2] In order to promote discussion at the Meeting, this Paper was printed, and advance copies were issued to Members on November 1st.

THE SHELLEY SOCIETY.
(*Original Prospectus, with slight revision.*)

THIS Society is started to gather the chief admirers of the Poet into a body which will work to do his memory honour, by meeting to discuss his writings, qualities, opinions, life, and doings; by getting his plays acted; by reprinting the rarest of his original editions; by facsimileing such of his MSS as may be accessible; by compiling a Shelley Lexicon or Concordance; by getting a Shelley Primer published; by generally investigating and illustrating his genius and personality from every side and in every detail; and by extending his influence.

The charm and power of Shelley as poet, essayist, letter-writer and man, are too widely acknowledged to need dwelling on here. No more attractive figure than his beams from the gallery of our literature. The present age is beginning to do justice to the high qualities of his genius, and it is but natural that those men and women who appreciate it should desire to band themselves into a Shelley Society, in which they can commune together and take steps to reach ends which, individually, they could not attain.

One of these is the performance of Shelley's plays. He himself wanted to have his *Cenci* on the stage, with Miss O'NEIL as Beatrice. MACREADY, after he had retired from the boards, declared he would come back to them if he had the chance of playing Count Cenci. Now the Shelley Society can get the play acted early next May. Miss ALMA MURRAY, whose charming performances of Constance and Colombe in Browning's *In a Balcony* and *Colombe's Birthday* have so delighted the Browning Society, has kindly promised to play Beatrice Cenci, and Mr. HERMANN VEZIN has been good enough to undertake Count Cenci. They will use their influence with other good actors to volunteer for the other parts. *Hellas* may perhaps follow *The Cenci* in November, 1886, as Dr. W. C. Selle is setting its choruses to music for the Society.

Many points to be discussed in Shelley's works and life, his religion, politics, sociology views of nature and art, mythology, metre, revisions, development, &c., &c., will occur to every student, as also the need of a reprint of his first editions, of old articles on him, and the facsimileing of his MSS. No one doubts that when a set of Shelley students get together, they will find plenty of work for their Shelley Society to do, and that their Papers and Discussions can be kept clear of any of the old *odium theologicum* and the like. Dispassionate treatment of all Shelley topics is now easy, and is consistent with the entire frankness of expression which the Society will always allow in its Meetings and publications.

It is proposed that the Committee consist of Shelley workers, Messrs. W. M. ROSSETTI, H. BUXTON FORMAN, T. J. WISE, TODHUNTER, B. DOBELL, and other students of Shelley, like the Rev. STOPFORD A. BROOKE, the Rev. W. A. HARRISON, Mr. ALFRED FORMAN, Mr. HENRY SWEET (who suggested the formation of a Shelley Society) and Dr. FURNIVALL (the founder of the Society), whose father knew and liked Shelley, as Shelley liked him. The number of the Committee will be twenty-four. This Committee will manage the Society till January 1887, and then suggest to Members the future Rules and Officers of the Society. (The Society is constituted for ten years only.) The Society's publishers are Messrs. REEVES and TURNER, of 196, Strand, London, W.C.; its printers, Messrs. R. CLAY and SONS, of Bread Street Hill, London, E.C., and Bungay, Suffolk.

The Society's Meetings will be held at University College, Gower Street, W.C., at 8 P.M., on the second Wednesday in March, April, May, November and December, 1886, &c. The first performance of *The Cenci* was at the Grand Theatre, Islington, on the afternoon of May 9th, 1886.

The Annual Subscription, which constitutes Membership, is One Guinea, due every 1st of January. Members' Names and Subscriptions should be sent at once to W. M. ROSSETTI, Esq., 5, Endsleigh Gardens, London, N.W., or to the Hon. Sec., JAMES STANLEY LITTLE, 76, Clarendon Road, Holland Park, W.

8*th December*, 1885.

The Society's Publications will be issued in Five (four *Ordinary* and one *Extra*), Series:—

Series I. will consist of the *Papers* read before the Society, and an Abstract of any which are not printed in full, together with Reports of the Discussions at the Society's Meetings. The *Abstracts* and *Reports* will appear in "*The Shelley Society's Note-Book*," which will be edited by the Honorary Secretary, and will contain Shelley "*Notes and Queries*" and 'News,' for both of which, contributions from Members are desired. The *Papers* and *Note-Book* will be issued both singly and in Parts. Each set will be formed into separate Parts and Volumes of convenient size.

Series II. will be a set of Type-Facsimile Reprints of the original editions of Shelley's works, with full bibliographical Introductions. A list of these will be found on page 7. Gifts of Reprints are much desired.

Series III. will consist of Reprints of the most important *Magazine Articles* on Shelley and his Works:

§ 1. *Biographical*, beginning with Hogg's seven important articles on "Shelley at Oxford," &c., in *The New Monthly Magazine*, 1832 and 1833.

§ 2. *Contemporary Criticisms* of Shelley's Works. (The abusive tone of most of these constitutes their main interest to Shelley students. The amusing ones in *The Gentleman's Magazine* of 1822 appeared in the Society's *Note-Book*, No. 2.)

§ 3. *Critical Articles* in later periodicals on Shelley and his Works. Though these will be mainly from journals of the last ten years (see the list on pages 8, 9), yet such Reviews as those of Shelley's *Posthumous Poems* in *The Edinburgh Review* of July 1824 (vol. xl. pp. 494-514, by Hazlitt), in the *Quarterly* of June 1826 (vol. xxxiv. pp. 148-153), in the *Metropolitan Quarterly Magazine* (No. 3), 1826, and *The Mirror* (vol. vii. pp. 215-217), 1826, and on Shelley in *The Censor*, 1829 (pp. 38-9, 49-51, 86), will not be excluded.

(The reproduction of Copyright Articles will of course depend on the consent of the copyright owners being obtained. The Committee trust that the generosity usual in like cases will be extended to the Shelley Society.)

Series IV. will be a *Miscellaneous* one, and will include an edition of *The Cenci* for the Society's performances of the play; Mr. Rossetti's *Memoir of Shelley*; *Shelley's Autobiography*; a *Shelley Primer* (by Mr. H. S. Salt); a *Concordance to Shelley's Poetical Works* (by the Society's Volunteers, and edited by Mr. F.S. Ellis); a *Word- and Subject-Index to his Prose Works and Letters*, and such other works as may hereafter be decided on.

Series V. (*Extra* Series) will include a cheap reprint of *Hellas*, for the Society's performance of the drama; cheap excerpts from some of the Society's larger works; photo-lithographic reprints of Shelley's original manuscripts, &c. Full details of this series will be found on p. 22.

PUBLICATIONS SUGGESTED.

Series I. *Papers and Note-Book.*

Papers.—Part I. The Inaugural Address of the Rev. Stopford A. Brooke, M.A., and other Papers of the Session 1886. [*At press.*

Note-Book.—Part I. Abstracts of the Discussions, Shelley "*Notes and Queries*," 'News,' &c. Nos. 1, 2, 3, 4, and 5 are already issued.

Series II. *Type-Facsimile Reprints of Shelley's Original Editions.*

1. *Adonais.* 4to. Pisa, 1821. Edited by THOMAS J. WISE. [*Issued.*

2. Shelley's Review of Hogg's *Memoirs of Prince Alexy Haimatoff* in the *Critical Review* for December 1814 (not in facsimile), with Prof. Dowden's Article on it.[1] Edited by THOMAS J. WISE. Crown 8vo. [*Issued.*

3. *Alastor.* Fcap. 8vo. 1816. Edited by BERTRAM DOBELL. [*Issued.*

4. *A Vindication of Natural Diet.* 12mo. 1813.[2] [*Issued.*

5. *Hellas, a Lyrical Drama.* 8vo. 1822. (Edited by THOMAS J. WISE. Presented by Mr. F. S. ELLIS.) [*Issued.*

6. *An Address to the Irish People.* 8vo. 1812. Edited by THOMAS J. WISE. Presented by Mr. WALTER B. SLATER. [*Ready immediately.*

7. *Epipsychidion.* 8vo. 1821. Presented by Mr. R. A. POTTS. [*Ready immediately.*

8. *The Necessity of Atheism.* 12mo. (Not dated, but 1811.) Edited and Presented by Mr. THOMAS J. WISE. [*Ready immediately.*

9. *Posthumous Fragments of Margaret Nicholson.* 4to. 1810. [*At press.*

10. *A Letter to Lord Ellenborough.* Crown 8vo. (Not dated, but 1812.) [*At press.*

11. *A Refutation of Deism.* 8vo. 1814. [*At press.*

12. *The Wandering Jew.* 8vo. Edited, with an Introduction, by BERTRAM DOBELL. [*Issued.*

13. *The Masque of Anarchy.* Fcap. 8vo. Written in 1819, first published in 1832. Edited by THOMAS J. WISE. [*Ready shortly.*

14. *Œdipus Tyrannus.* 8vo. 1820.

15. *Proposals for an Association of Philanthropists.* 8vo. (Not dated, but 1812.)

16. *A Proposal for putting Reform to the Vote.* 8vo. 1817.

17. *Rosalind and Helen.* 8vo. 1819.

18. *Prometheus Unbound.* 8vo. 1821.

19. *Laon and Cythna.* 8vo. 1818. With Shelley's MS. alterations of it into *The Revolt of Islam.* Edited by H. BUXTON FORMAN. [*Preparing.*

20. *Queen Mab.* Crown 8vo. 1813. With Shelley's MS. alterations. Edited by H. BUXTON FORMAN.

21. *Zastrozzi.* 12mo. 1810.

22. *St. Irvyne, or the Rosicrucian.* 12mo. 1811.

23. *Posthumous Poems.* 8vo. 1822.

24. *Essays, Letters from Abroad, &c.* 2 vols. Crown 8vo. 1841.

---

[1] From "Some Early Writings of Shelley," in *The Contemporary Review*, September, 1884.
[2] 500 copies of the cheap reprint of this tract have been presented to the Society by Mr. W. E. A. AXON.

Series III. *Magazine Articles.*

(Many of the most important contributions to Shelley Biography are to be found in Periodical Literature. The following are those chiefly needed to fill up the gaps in the story of the Poet's life, and to correct the many inaccuracies of Hogg, Medwin, and other of his earlier biographers.)

SECTION 1.—*Biographical.*

PART 1.—Statements by writers personally acquainted with Shelley.

Edited, with an Introduction, by Thomas J. Wise.

With two Portraits. Now at press.

1. "Percy Bysshe Shelley," in *Stockdale's Budget*, 1826-7.
2. Hogg's "Shelley at Oxford,"[1] in *The New Monthly Magazine*, January, February, April, July, October, and December, 1832, pp. 90-96, 136-144, 343-352, 65-73, 321-330, 505-513.
3. Hogg's "The History of Percy Bysshe Shelley's Expulsion from Oxford," in *The New Monthly Magazine*, for May, 1833, pp. 17-29.
4. "A Newspaper Editor's Reminiscences," in *Fraser*, No. cxxviii. June, 1841, pp. 699-710.
5. Peacock's "Memoirs of Shelley," in *Fraser*, No. cccxlii., June, 1858 pp. 643-659; No. ccclxi., January, 1860, pp. 92-109; No. ccclxiii., March, 1860, pp. 301-319; No. ccclxv., May, 1860, p. 738; and No. ccclxxxvii. March, 1862, pp. 343-346.
6. "Shelley, by One who Knew Him," by Thornton Hunt, in *The Atlantic Monthly*, February, 1863, pp. 184-204.

The Committee would be glad if members who may possess the holographs of any of Shelley's Letters printed in either of the above articles, would kindly allow the editor to collate them.

PART II.—Statements by later writers.

1. "Notes on Shelley's Birthplace," by W. Hale White, in *Macmillan's Magazine*, No. 233, vol. xxxix. pp. 461-465.
2. "On the Drowning of Shelley," by R. H. Horne, in *Fraser*, Nov. 1870, pp. 618-625.
3. "Shelley in 1812—13: An Unpublished Poem," by W. M. Rossetti, in *The Fortnightly Review*, January, 1871, pp. 67-85.
4. "Shelley's Last Days," by Dr. Garnett, in *The Fortnightly Review*, June 1, 1878, pp. 850-866.
5. "Improvvisatore Sgricci in Relation to Shelley," by H. Buxton Forman, in *The Gentleman's Magazine*, January, 1880, pp. 115-123.
6. "Shelley's Life near Spezzia, his Death and Burials," by H. Buxton Forman, in *Macmillan's Magazine*, No. 247, May, 1880, pp. 43-58.
7. "Shelley and Mary," in *The Edinburgh Review*, No. 320, October, 1882, pp. 472-507.

---

[1] The six articles under this title ("Shelley at Oxford"), and the supplementary article recounting the Expulsion of Shelley and himself from Oxford, contributed by Hogg to *The New Monthly Magazine*, in 1832 and 1833, form perhaps the most valuable portion of the two volumes which Hogg afterwards issued in 1858.

Series III. SECTION 2.—*Contemporary Criticisms* of Shelley and his Works.

1. Review of "Zastrozzi" in *The Critical Review*. November, 1810, vol. xxi. 3rd series, 1811.
2. ,, "St. Irvyne" in *The British Critic*, January, 1811.
3. ,, "Poems by Victor and Cazire" in *The Poetical Register*, vol. viii., 1810-11, p. 617.
4. ,, "Poems by Victor and Cazire" in *The British Critic*, April, 1811, vol. xxxvii. p. 408.
5. ,, "Queen Mab" in *The Theological Inquirer*, 1815.
6. ,, Poems in *The Mirror*, 1819.
7. ,, "Alastor" in *Blackwood's Magazine*, November, 1819.
8. ,, "Laon and Cythna," "The Revolt of Islam" in *The Quarterly*, No. xlii., September, 1819, pp. 460-471 (and "Rosalind and Helen," p. 470).
9. ,, "Rosalind and Helen," and "Alastor" in *Blackwood's Magazine*, June and Nov., 1819; and "Adonais," in Dec., 1821.
10. ,, "The Cenci" in *The Literary Gazette*, No. 167, April 1, 1820, pp. 209-210.
11. ,, "Prometheus Unbound" in *The Literary Gazette*, No. 190, September 9, 1820, pp. 580-582.
12. ,, "The Cenci" in *The New Monthly Magazine*, May, 1820.
13. ,, "The Cenci" in *The London Magazine*, No. 5, May, 1820.
14. "*The Honeycomb*," No. 9. Saturday, August 12, 1820. "Portraits of the Metropolitan Poets," No. iii. Mr. Percy Bysshe Shelley pp. 65-71.
15. Review of "Queen Mab" in *The Literary Gazette*, No. 226, May 19, 1821, pp. 305-308.
16. ,, "Epipsychidion," in *The Gossip*, June, 1821.
17. ,, "Adonais" in *The Literary Gazette*, December 8, 1821, pp. 772-773.
18. ,, "Prometheus Unbound" in *The Quarterly*, No. xli., December, 1821, pp. 168-180.
19. Leigh Hunt's 'Reviews' in *The Examiner*.

Series III. SECTION 3.

The most important *critical* articles—not necessarily excluding *reviews*—which have been contributed to later periodicals.

1. "The Life and Poetry of Shelley," by David Masson, in *Macmillan's Magazine*, June, 1860, pp. 338-350.
2. "The Poems of Shelley," in *The North British Review*, No. cv., October, 1870, pp. 30-58.
3. "Shelley's Metaphysics," by A. Cordery, in the *Dark Blue*, June, 1872, pp. 478-488.
4. "Shelley's 'Prometheus Unbound,'" by Arthur Clive, in *The Gentleman's Magazine*, No. lxxi., April, 1874, pp. 421-437.
5. Mr. W. M. Rossetti's two Lectures on Shelley, in the *Dublin University Magazine*, February and March, 1878, pp. 138-155, 262-277.

6. "Some Thoughts on Shelley," by Stopford A. Brooke, in *Macmillan's Magazine*, No. 248, June, 1880, pp. 124-135.

7. "The Prometheus of Æschylus and of Shelley," by the Rev. W. A. O'Conor, B.A., in *The Manchester Quarterly*, No. i., January, 1882, pp. 29-45.

8. "Shelley as a Teacher," by H. S. Salt, in *Temple Bar*, No. 264, November, 1882, pp. 365-377.

9. "A Note on Shelley," by James Thomson (B.V.) in *Progress*, vol. iii., No. 2, February, 1884, pp. 113-117.

10. "Some Early Writings of Shelley," by Professor Dowden, in *The Contemporary Review*, September, 1884, pp. 383-396.

11. "Shelley's Philosophical View of Reform," by Professor Dowden, in *The Fortnightly Review*, November 1886, No. ccxxxix., New Series, pp. 543-562.

Series IV. *Miscellaneous.*

1. "A Shelley Bibliography." Part I. Edited by H. Buxton Forman. (This work is published by Reeves and Turner.) [*Issued.*

2. "A Memoir of Shelley" (reprinted from Mr. Rossetti's edition of his Works), with a fresh Preface by W. M. Rossetti, and a full *Index*. [*Issued.*

3. "The Cenci": a cheap edition for the Society's performance of the Tragedy in May, 1886, with an etched portrait of Beatrice, an Introduction by Alfred Forman and H. Buxton Forman, and a Prologue by Dr. John Todhunter. [*Issued.*

4. "A Shelley Primer." By H. S. Salt, M.A. (Messrs. Reeves and Turner, 196, Strand, W.C., published this early in 1887, and the Society took a copy for each of its Members.) [*Issued.*

5. The Pianoforte Score of Dr. W. C. Selle's Choruses and Recitatives, composed for the Society's performance of Shelley's *Hellas* in November, 1886: with an Introduction by the Composer. Imperial 8vo. *Wrappers.* [*Issued.*

6. "Shelley's Autobiography:" *Cor Cordium.* A collection of all passages (poetry or prose) by Shelley relating to himself and his works, with annotations by Wm. Michael Rossetti. [*Preparing.*

7. "A Concordance to Shelley's *Poetical Works*," and "a *General* and *Subject* Index to his *Prose Works* and *Letters.*" Mr. F. S. Ellis has been good enough to undertake the editorship of these. Mrs. H. Buxton Forman has kindly placed her material for the former portion of this work at the Society's disposal. The Committee ask for volunteer help in both portions. Specimens are ready. Offers of help are to be sent to Mr. F. S. Ellis, The Red House, Chelston, Torquay. [*Preparing.*

8. A reprint, in one volume, of Peacock's *Four Ages of Poetry*, and Shelley's *Defence of Poetry*.

9. "A Memoir of Shelley," by Leigh Hunt.

10. Extracts from books relating to Shelley, compiled under the superintendence of H. Buxton Forman.

Members are invited to forward suggestions for such additional Publications as they may consider it desirable for the Society to produce.

NOTE.—A few Large-Paper copies (Quarto size) of some of the Society's Publications have been privately printed; they can be obtained by Members upon application to Mr. Bertram Dobell, 66, Queen's Crescent, Haverstock Hill, London, N.W.

MEMBERS.

Abbott, T. C., Eastlegh, Queen's Road, Bowdon, Manchester.
Abercrombie, W., The Manor House, Ashton-upon-Mersey.
Alexander, P. F., 5, Ship Street, Oxford.
Alexander, Professor W. J., care of Reeves & Turner, 196, Strand, W.C.
Allan, Hugh, 33, Crescent Road, Plumstead, Kent.
Angell, E. A., c/o Messrs. Angell and Webster, Cleveland, Ohio, U.S.A.
Arkwright, Wm., Sutton, Scarsdale, Chesterfield.
Armour, George A., 116, Home Insurance Buildings, Chicago, U.S.A.
Ashbee, C. R. A., 53, Bedford Square London, W.C.
Axon, Wm. E. A., 66, Murray Street, Higher Broughton, Manchester.
Aylward, F. Grahame, 51, Westmoreland Road, Newcastle-on-Tyne.
Badley, J. H., Trinity College, Cambridge.
Baddeley, St. Clair, 5, Albert Hall Mansions, Kensington Gore, S.W.
Bain, Andrew, 17, Athole Gardens, Kilvinside, Glasgow.
Bangs, Lemuel W., 188, Fleet Street, London, E.C.
Barnard, Mrs. Jas. Munson, Milton Hill, Milton, Mass., U.S.A.
Beaumont, Hubert, 144, Piccadilly, London, W.
Becker, Mrs. C., 9, Museum Mansions, Great Russell Street, London, W.C.
Bell, J. M., Heddan House, Isleworth, London, W.
Bell, Rev. Canon, D.D., Cheltenham.
Bell, Matthew, Temple Works, Cursitor Street, London, E.C.
Bell, Mrs. J. M., 24, Chestnut Street, Boston, Mass., U.S.A.
Bennett, Miss F. E., Ogontz P. O., Montgomery Co., Pa., U.S.A.
Berdoe, E., Tynemouth House, Victoria Park Gate, London, E.
Best, John Vincent, 42, Lansdowne Gardens, South Lambeth, S.W.
Bierstadt, Edward H., 2, Wall Street, New York City, U.S.A.
Binney, Mrs., Hillfield, Hampstead, London, N.
Binns, J. Arthur, 31, Manor Road, Bradford.
Bird, Miss Laura, 105, Great Russell Street, London, W.C.
Bird, W. S., 105, Great Russell Street, London, W.C.
Birnstingl, Avigdor, 18, Old Broad Street, London, E.C.
Black, T. Fraser, 7, Mount View Road, Crouch Hill, London, N.
Bland, Hubert, Bowater Crescent, Woolwich Hill.
Blind, Miss Mathilde, 27, Manchester Street, London, W.
Booker, John L., 128, Piccadilly, London, W.
Boston Athenæum, c/o Messrs. Trübner & Co., 57 & 59, Ludgate Hill, E.C.
Boston Public Library, c/o Messrs. Trübner, 57 & 59, Ludgate Hill.
Bowring, Walter A., Meadow Lodge, Kingston Hill, Surrey.
Bradley, Mrs. Jerram, 3, Park Terrace, Northampton.

Bradley, Miss Emily T., Deanery, Westminster, London, S.W.
Brandl, Professor Dr. A., 3, Stephangasse, Prag, Bohemia.
Brice, Seward, 5, Bedford Square, London, W.C.
Britton, John James, Heath House, Alcester, Warwickshire.
Brooke, Rev. Stopford A., 1, Manchester Square, London, W.
Brooksbank, Mrs. Thos., 7, Chester Place, Regent's Park, London, N.W.
Brown, John, 2, St. James's Place, Hillhead, Glasgow.
Browning, Oscar, King's College, Cambridge.
Bucke, R. Maurice, M.D., Asylum for the Insane, London, Ont., Canada.
Burd, Mrs. T. H., Campion House, Shrewsbury.
Burgess, Mrs. Bougbey, 78, Tyrwhitt Road, St. John's, S.E.
Burgin, Geo. B., 7, Dryden Road, Bush Hill Park, Enfield, London, N.
Butler, R. F., London Institution, Finsbury Circus, London, E.C.
Cabot, Mrs. Arthur T., 3, Marlborough Street, Boston, Mass., U.S.A.
Call, Major, R.E., 26, Cheyne Walk, Chelsea, London, S.W.
Call, Mrs. C. F., 26, Cheyne Walk, Chelsea, London, S.W.
Call, W. M. W., 9, Addison Gardens, Kensington, London, W.
Call, Mrs. W., 9, Addison Gardens, Kensington, London, W.
Campbell, J. Dykes, 29, Albert Hall Mansions, Kensington Gore, S.W.
Candy, Hugh, University Hall, Gordon Square, London, W.C.
Carter, William, Parkeston, Dorset.
Cass, A. M., Lime Grove, Longsight, Manchester.
Cave, Geo., 15, Montague Road, Richmond, London, S.W.
Cawthorn, James, 19, Selborne Road, Brighton.
Cazalet, Mrs. W. Clement, Grenehurst, Dorking, Surrey.
Chawner, G., King's College, Cambridge.
Child, Addison, Childwold, St. Lawrence Co., New York.
Clarke, B.A., Hampden House, Crouch End, London, N.
Clough, William, 55, High Street, Chorlton-upon-Medlock.
Clulow, George, 51, Belsize Avenue, Hampstead, London, N.W.
Coates, Miss A. E., Hart Street, Henley-on-Thames.
Cobden, Miss, 17, Canfield Gardens, West Hampstead, London, N.W.
Coffin, T. W., 22, Upper Park Road, Haverstock Hill, London, N.W.
Coles, C. B. Cowper, 95, Wigmore Street, London, W.
Comins, Herbert, Queen's Cottage, Chingford, Essex.
Comyn, Mrs. M., 12, Aldridge Road Villas, Bayswater, London, W.
Cook, Sam., 14, Gloucester Road, Queen's Road, Finsbury Park, N.
Cooper, F. S., Royal Grammar School, Lancaster.
Craig, W. J., 18, Edwardes Square, London, W.
Craik, G. Lillie, 29 & 30, Bedford Street, Covent Garden, London, W.C.
Crane, Walter, Beaumont Lodge, Shepherds Bush, London, W.
Craufurd, W. D., 41, Cadogan Terrace, Sloane Street, London, S.W.
Crouch, E. Heath, East London, Cape Colony, South Africa.
Cyriax, Jules, 33, Douglas Road, Canonbury, London, N.
Dale, Andrew, 12, The Terrace, Camberwell Park, London, S.E.
Dallas-Glyn, Mrs., 13, Mount Street, Grosvenor Square, London, W.
Davenport, Mrs. Mary S., 108, Sinclair Road, West Kensington, W.
Davey, Richard, 14, Rathbone Place, London, W.C.
Dawson, Miss, 30, Devonshire St., Portland Place, London, W.
Denny, Daniel, jun., 31, Little's Block, Cambridge, Mass. U.S.A.
Donald, T. F., 146, Buchanan Street, Glasgow, N.B.
Dillon, Arthur, Tripp Hill, Fittleworth, Pulborough.

Dobell, Bertram, 66, Queen's Crescent, Haverstock Hill, London, N.W.
Donkin, H. B., 60, Upper Berkeley Street, London, W.
Dowdeswell, Chas., Brantwood, Macaulay Road, Clapham Common, S.W.
Draper, E. Herbert, 52, Doughty Street, London, W.C.
Druitt, Miss Emily, 447, Mile End Road, Bow, London, E.
Dyer, Prof. Louis, 104, Mount Auburn Street, Cambridge, Mass., U.S.A.
Eckenstein, T., 29, Douglas Road, London, N.
Edgcumbe, R., 33, Tedworth Square, Chelsea, London, S.W.
Edmiston, Miss E., 4, Endsleigh Street, Euston Road, London, W.C.
Ellis, F. S., The Red House, Chelston, Torquay.
Emrys-Jones, A., M.D., Oak Hill, Fallowfield, Manchester.
Fagan, Mrs., 26, Manchester Square, London, W.
Farren, J. W., 8, Lansdowne Road, Clapham Road, London, S.W.
Fea, J. F., War Office, Pall Mall, London, S.W.
Field, Michael, care of Messrs. Baker and Sons, The Mall, Clifton.
Firth, E. Harding, Leigh Side, Leigh Woods, Clifton, Bristol.
Forman, Alfred, 7, Holbeck Road, Stockwell, London, S.W.
Forman, George, 1, Upper Phillimore Place, Kensington, London, W
Forman, H. Buxton, 46, Marlborough Hill, St. John's Wood, N.W.
Forman, Mrs., 5, Wilton Terrace, Camberwell Grove, London, S.E.
Foster, Fred. W., Neckinger Mills, Bermondsey, London, S.E.
Foss, G. R., 26, Great Ormond Street, London, W. C.
Fothergill, Miss Alice, 109, Abbey Road, London, N.W.
Fountain, Alfred, Highfield, Hillingdon, Uxbridge, Middlesex.
Franks, Walter J., Highview, Upper Norwood, London, S.E.
Frederickson, Charles W., 741, Lexington Avenue, New York City, U.S.A.
Frederickson, Mrs. C. W., 741, Lexington Avenue, New York City, U.S.A.
Frost, H. F., 6, Southampton Street, Strand, London, W.C.
Fry, R. E. (King's College), 3, Pear Hill, Cambridge.
Furnivall, Dr. F. J., 3, St. George's Sq., Primrose Hill, N.W. (*Treasurer*.)
Galway, John, care of H. S. Sotheran & Co., 136, Strand, London, W.C.
Garden, Hugh, Heathcote, Lichfield Road, Kew Gardens, London, S.W.
Gardner, Mrs. John L., 152, Beacon Street, Boston, Mass., U.S.A.
Gibbs, J. W. M., 34, Southampton Road, Haverstock Hill, London, N.W.
Goulden, W., 45, St. Peter's Street, Canterbury.
Graham, Thomas, Laurel Bank, 20, Hilldrop Road, London, N.
Gray, George, Blairtoun Park, Rutherglen, N.B.
Green, T. E., 106, St. Paul's Road, Camden Square, London, N.W.
Grierson, G. G., St. Peter's College, Cambridge.
Grigsby, W. E., LL.D., 49, Chancery Lane, London, W.C.
Griswold, D. P., 47, Brattle Street, Cambridge, Mass., U.S.A.
Guildhall Library, London, E.C. (W. H. Overall, Librarian.)
Hadrill, Hy. Jno., 53, Belsize Avenue, London, N.W.
Hainsworth, L., 118, Bowling Old Lane, Bradford, Yorkshire.
Hales, Prof. J. W., 1, Oppidans Road, Primrose Hill, London, N.W.
Hall, C. Gordon, Union Club, Trafalgar Square, London, W.
Hall, Richard Thomas, care of James Dalgaison, Esq., General Post Office, Sydney, N.S.W.
Hanson, E., 42, York Terrace, Regent's Park, N.W.
Harden, W. Tyas, Hamlet Road, Upper Norwood, London, S.W.
Harrison, Rev. W. A., St. Ann's Vicarage, S. Lambeth, London, S.W.
Hart, Horace, Controller, University Press, Oxford.

Harvard College, c/o Trübner & Co., 57, Ludgate Hill, London, E.C.
Hatchard, Mrs. H. Gibbons, Sylvanus Villa, 211, Maida Vale, London, W.
Hatchard, Miss Marion L., Sylvanus Villa, 211, Maida Vale, London, W.
Hawthorne, Miss, c/o George Temple, Esq., 7, High Street, Bloomsbury
Haynes, W. B., 137, King's Cross Road, London, W.C.
Hemery, Mrs., Charles, Gladsmuir, Barnet, Herts.
Hibbs, Reginald R., 13, St. Lawrence Road, North Kensington, W.
Higginson, 3rd. George, 32, Little's Block, Cambridge, Mass. U.S.A.
Hill, Mrs. Eardley, 6, Oxford Square, Hyde Park, London, W.
Hillier, A. C., 6, Phillimore Gardens, Kensington, London, W.
Hole, Jas., 1, Great College Street, Westminster, London, S.W.
Holyoake, Percy, Fairbourne, King's Road, Clapham Park, London, S.W.
Home, F. Wyville, 1, Gordon Villas, Woodside, London, S.E.
Hope, Miss, 14, Airlie Gardens, Campden Hill, London, N.
Hora, Whinfield, 16, The Terrace, Peckham Road, London, S.E.
Horniman, Emslie John, Surrey Mount, Forest Hill, London, S.E.
Horsford, Miss Lilian, 27 Craigie Street, Cambridge, Mass. U.S.A.
Howell, F. F., St. John's College, Cambridge.
Hudson, John E., 334, Marlborough Street, Boston, Mass.
Hueffer, Mrs., 72, Elsham Road, Addison Road, Kensington, London, W.
Hugell, J. Snell, 24, Regent's Square, London, W.C.
Hughes, Arthur S., 37, Old Jewry, London, E.C.
Hutt, A. Granger, 8, Oxford Road, Kilburn, London, N.W.
Hutt, Charles, 30, Hargrave Park Road, Junction Road, London, N.
Ingram, John H., Howard House, Stoke Newington Green, London, N.
Jack, Adolphus A., 10, The University, Glasgow.
Jackson, Miss, North London Collegiate School for Girls, Sandall Road, N.W.
Jacob, H. P. (of Bombay), Elm Grove, Dawlish.
Jarvis, J. W. Junr., 19, Bardolph Road, Tufnell Park, London, N.
Jersey, The Countess of, 3, Great Stanhope Street, Mayfair, London, W.
Johnson, Charles Plumptre, 9, New Square, Lincoln's Inn, W.C.
Jones, Hy. A.. The Hill House, Chalfont St. Peter, Slough, Bucks.
Jones, Mrs. Charles, Jesmond Dene, Newcastle-on-Tyne.
Joyce, Miss A., 27, Park Road, Haverstock Hill, London, N.W.
Justice, Philip M., 55, Chancery Lane, London, W.C.
Kendal, Mrs., 145, Harley Street, London, W.
Kerr, Mrs., Northbank, Altrincham, Cheshire.
Kerr, Mrs. Alexr., 19, Warwick Road, South Kensington, London, S.W.
Kerr, Mrs. William, Glan William, Tan-y-Bwlch, Merioneth.
Kloos, Willem, Hemonystraat, 13, Amsterdam, Holland.
Knight, H. J., 30, George Street, Hampstead Road, London, N.W.
Lassiter, Francis Rives, Tavern Club, 1, Park Square, Boston, Mass., U.S.A.
Latham, Mrs. G., 18, Arundel Gardens, London, W.
Lawson, H. L., M.P., 32, Grosvenor Square, London, W.
Lee, A. Collingwood, Waltham Abbey, Essex.
Lee, Sidney L., 26, Brondesbury Villas, Kilburn, London, N.W.
Le Gallienne, Richard, Woodstock, Prenton Lane, Birkenhead.
Leveson, E. J., Cluny, Anerley, London, S.E.
Levy, Jonas, 55, Tavistock Square, London, W.C.
Lewis, Enoch, c/o The Pennsylvania R. R. Co., 233, South Fourth Street,
    Philadelphia, Pa., U.S.A.
Lewis, W. B., African Steamship Company, 31, James Street, Liverpool.

Lindsay, W. A., St. Peter's College, Cambridge.
Linton, Mrs. Lynn, Queen Anne's Mansions, St. James's Park, S.W.
Lisle, Miss Underwood, 5, Cornwall Residences, Clarence Gate, W. (*Hon. Sec.*)
Little, Jas. Stanley, 76, Clarendon Road, Holland Park, London, W.
Locke, F. S., 1, New Court, St. John's College, Cambridge.
Lodge, Mrs. Henry Cabot, 65, Mount Vernon Street, Boston, Mass. U.S.A.
Lodge, Mrs. J. E., 31, Beacon Street, Boston, Mass. U.S.A.
Lounsbury, Prof. T. R., New Haven, Conn., U.S.A.
Low, Miss Marie A., 60, Park Road, Haverstock Hill, London, N.W.
Lowell, Hon. J. Russell, 40, Clarges Street, Piccadilly, London, W.
Lyndon, Miss Eleanor, 186, Adelaide Road, South Hampstead, N.W.
Lyster, Thomas W., 10, Harcourt Terrace, Dublin.
Macalister, Miss, Alcester, Warwickshire.
Macey, F. H., 268, Strand, London, W.C.
MacGeorge, B., 19, Woodside Crescent, Glasgow.
MacKee, Thomas J. 237 West 24th Street, New York City, U.S.A.
Macleod, Miss E., 17, Gloucester Walk, Campden Hill, Kensington, W.
Macmillan, Alexander, 29, Bedford Street, Covent Garden, London, W.C.
Maier, Gustav, Bankcommandite, Gustav Maier & Co., Frankfurt-am-Main, Deutschland.
Main, David M., 18, Exchange Square, Glasgow.
Manchester Public Free Libraries (C. W. Sutton, Esq., Librarian).
Marillier, H. C., Peterhouse, Cambridge.
Marsh, B. J., Devoncroft, Fairfield, Kingston-on-Thames, London, S.W.
Mathie, Mrs. J. Forlong, 49, Comeragh Road, West Kensington, London, W.
Matthew, Miss, 14, St. Thomas Road, South Hackney, London, N.
Matthews, W. H., c/o Messrs. Matthews & Brooke, Sun Buildings, Bradford.
Mauchlen, Rev. J., Aden House, Ennerdale Road, Kew, London, S.W.
Maw, William, Secretary Bradford Infirmary, Bradford, Yorkshire.
May, Mrs. S. L., Macro's Cottage, Burnham Beeches. Slough.
McArthur, A. G., Raleigh Hall, Brixton Rise, London, S.W.
Meller, Miss, Rothley Villa, Macaulay Road, Clapham, London, S.W.
Mercer, F. J., North Warren, Gainsborough.
Meriscord, H., 27, Russell Street, London, W.C.
Millar, A., Hollyhurst, Clapham Common, London, S.W.
Milligan, Miss A., 13, Cromwell Grove, W. Kensington Park, London, W.
Milner, George, 59a, Morley Street, Manchester.
Monkhouse, A. N., Bexton Road, Knutsford.
Moore, Mrs., Wedderburn House, Hampstead, London, N.W.
Morgan, E. Delmas, Union Club, Trafalgar Square, London, S.W.
Morrison, G. E., care of W. Earle, 8, Cathcart Road, S. Kensington, S.W.
Mosely, B. L, 55, Tavistock Square, London, W.C.
Mugliston, Rev. John, Newick House, Cheltenham.
Muir, James, 27, Huntley Gardens, Glasgow.
Muir, Wm., 9, Angel Place, Edmonton, London, N.
Munn, George F., Arts Club, Hanover Square, London, W.
Murray, Miss Alma, 7, Holbeck Road. Stockwell, London, S.W.
Murray, Mrs., Brambledown, Crouch Hill, London, N.
Murray, Frank, Moray House, Derby.
Napier, Prof. A. S., Headington Hill, Oxford.
National Library of Ireland, Dublin.
Neate, Mrs., 53, Belsize Park, London, N.W.

Nesmith, H. E. jun., 28, South Street, New York, U.S.A.
Newell, E. J., The College, Dumfries Place, Cardiff.
Nichols, George L. jnr., 146, Broadway, New York, U.S.A.
Nicólls, Jasper H. E., Art Club, Bennet Park, Blackheath, London, S.E.
Norman, Henry, 10, Northumberland Street, London, W.C.
Oakeshott, J. F., New Barnet, Middlesex.
O'Connor, T. B., 168, Piccadilly, London, W.
Offor, George, Peak Hill Villa, Sydenham, S E.
Overton, Mrs. A. M., 246, Portsdown Road, Maida Hill, London, W.
Owens, Mrs., Holestone, Doagh, Belfast.
Pagliardini, Signor Tito, 75, Upper Berkeley Street, Portman Square, W.
Palmer, W. J., 11, Pemberton Gardens, Upper Holloway, London, N.
Parker, Robert John, 27, Brunswick Gardens, Kensington, London, W.
Parkes, W. Kineton, Summerfield Crescent, Edgbaston, Birmingham.
Parks, Frank, Oberlin, Kansas, U.S.A.
Paton, Sir Joseph Noël, R.S.A., 33, George Square, Edinburgh.
Payne, John, 5, Lansdowne Place, Brunswick Square, London, W.C.
Peirce, Prof. Jas. Mills, 4, Kirkland Place, Cambridge, Mass., U.S.A.
Peile, G. Greenwood, Shotley Bridge, County Durham.
Perkins, Rev. Thos., Grammar School, Shaftesbury, Dorset.
Perry, Thomas Sergeant, 312, Marlborough Street, Boston, Mass., U.S.A.
Phillips, Rev. T. Lloyd, The Abbey, Beckenham, Kent.
Pinsent, Hume C., 6, Hyde Park Mansions, Marylebone Road, N.W.
Ploetz, R. A., Eton College, Windsor, Berks.
Pocock, Mrs. Alfred, Charisholme, Palace Road, Streatham Hill, S.W.
Posnett, Prof. H. Macaulay, Auckland University, New Zealand.
Potts, R. A., 26, South Audley Street, London, W.
Power, Robert, Moorhead Villas, Shipley, Yorks.
Power, P. le Poer, Winter's Buildings, 32, St. Ann's Street, Manchester.
Prentice, Mrs. Ridley, Wedderburn House, Hampstead, London, N.W.
Preston, Herbert P., 88, Eaton Place, London, S.W.
Preston, Mrs., 88, Eaton Place, London, S.W.
Preston, Sydney E., 88, Eaton Place, London, S.W.
Prideaux, Colonel W. P., 4, Alipore Lane, Calcutta.
Radford, Charles H., West Axton, Horrabridge, South Devon.
Radford, Ernest W., 9, The Terrace, Hammersmith, London, W.
Radford, George R., 2, Addison Road, Bedford Park, London, W.
Read, Carveth, 38, Leamington Road Villas, Westbourne Park, London, W.
Read, Miss Edith, 1, St. George's Square, Primrose Hill, London, N.W.
Rees, J. Rogers, Brecon Old Bank House, Cardiff.
Reeves, W., 196, Strand, London, W.C.
Reid, James, Chapel Allerton, Leeds.
Reinagle, Mrs., 15, Twyford Place, Tiverton, N. Devon.
Revell, Wm. F., 58, Oxford Gardens, Notting Hill, London, W.
Rhys, Ernest, 59, Cheyne Walk, Chelsea, London, S.W.
Richards, W. R., 2, Marlborough Street, Boston, Mass., U.S.A.
Richmond, John, Silverbank Villa, Cambuslang, Glasgow.
Riesco, E., Wool Exchange, Coleman Street, London, E.C.
Roe, Bassett, 25, Richmond Road, Thornhill Crescent, London, N.
Ross, A. G., 8, Ashburn Place, Cromwell Road, Kensington, London, W.
Ross, R. B., 8, Ashburn Place, Cromwell Road, S.W.
Rossetti, Wm. M., 5, Endsleigh Gardens, Euston Road, N.W. (*Chairman*.)

Rossiter, J. J., 12, Abbot's Walk, Forbury Gardens, Reading.
Rowley, Charles, The Glen, Harperbury, Manchester.
Russell, Earl, Ferishtah, Hampton, Middlesex.
Ruston, Miss, Monks' Manor, Lincoln.
Sabin, Frank T., 10, Garrick Street, London, W.C.
Salt, H. S., Tilford, Farnham, Surrey.
Samelson, A., M.D., 15, John Street, Manchester.
Sampson, Gerald N., Exeter College, Oxford.
Sarrazin, Gabriel, Lycée de Nancy, Meurthe-et-Moselle, France.
Schlengemann, E., 8, Wilberforce Road, Finsbury Park, London, N.
Scoffern, Mrs. Alice, 107, Clapham Road, London, S.W.
Scott, William Bell, Penkill Castle, Girvan, Ayrshire, N.B.
Scott, R. P., 135, East India Road, Poplar, London, E.
Sears, Miss Mary, 85, Mount Vernon Street, Boston, Mass., U.S.A.
Seawell, Miss M., c/o Miss Burrow, 29, Addison Road, Kensington, W.
Sebley, F. J., 7, Pulling Terrace, Cambridge.
Selle, W. C., Mus. Doc., 5, Old Palace Terrace, Richmond, S.W. (*Hon. Member.*)
Sellon, Miss M. G., The Hall, Sydenham, London, S.E.
Sharp, Wm., 46, Talgarth Road, West Kensington, London, W.
Shaw, George Bernard, 36, Osnaburgh Street, London, N.W.
Sheldon, Edw. W., University Club, Madison Square, New York, U.S.A.
Shelley, Sir Percy F., Bart., Boscombe Manor, Bournemouth, Hants.
Shelley, Lady, Boscombe Manor, Bournemouth, Hants.
Shipley, Conway, Kelly College, Tavistock, Devon.
Shorter, Clement K., 2, Gresley Road, Hornsey Lane, London, N.
Sickert, Mrs. E. M., 54, Broadhurst Gardens, South Hampstead, N.W.
Silsbee, Edward, Salem, Mass., U.S.A.
Simpson, Mrs. Jane H., 8, Park Place Villas, London, W.
Skipwith, Grey Hubert, 4, Upper College Street, Nottingham.
Slark, John, 12, Busby Place, Camden Road, London, N.W.
Slater, Walter B., 249, Camden Road, London, N.
Smart, Miss M. 8, Derby Villas, Forest Hill, London, S.E.
Smith, G. A., 92, Carleton Road, Tufnell Park, London, N.
Smith, W. J., 41. 43, North Street, Brighton.
Smithson, Mrs. Edward W., 13, Lendal, York.
Somerset, A., Frimley, Surrey.
Sotheran, Messrs. Henry, and Co., 136, Strand, London, W.C.
Stanley, Miss Sara. 3, Stirling Mansions, Compayne Gardens, South Hampstead, N.W.
Stevenson, A. L., St. Andrewes, Clevedon.
Stirling, James, 14, Rugby Road, Belfast.
Stock, Elliot, Fern Lodge, Millfield Lane, Highgate Rise, London, N.
Stockley, W. F., University of New Brunswick, Fredericton, N. B., Canada.
Stokes, J. Scott, Kew Cottage, Caterham, Surrey.
Story, John B., 24, Lower Baggot Street, Dublin.
Stringham, Professor Irving, University of California, Berkeley, California, U.S.A.
Sullivan, T. R., 10, Charles Street, Boston, Mass, U.S.A.
Sutton, Albert, 130, Portland Street, Manchester.
Sweet, Hy., Mansfield Cottage, Heath Street, Hampstead, London, N.W.

Sweetland, Mrs., 18, Nottingham Place, London, W.
Symons, J. H., 9, Alwyne Place, London, N.
Tee, W. F., Blagrave Street, Reading.
Tegetmeier, W. B., 16, Alexandra Grove, North Finchley, London, N.W,
Tegetmeier, Miss, 16, Alexandra Grove, North Finchley, London, N.W.
Tegetmeier, Miss Ida, 16, Alexandra Grove, North Finchley, London, N.W.
Tempest, Adolphus Vane, 112, Bond Street, London, W.
Thicknesse, Ralph, 1, Stone Buildings, Lincoln's Inn, London, W.C.
Thin, G. T., 32, Grange Road, Edinburgh.
Thompson, Chas. E., care of Messrs. P. Putnam's Sons, 27, King William Street, London, W.C.
Thorn-Drury, G., Lamb Buildings, Temple, London, E.C.
Thwaites, E. W., 16, Durham Villas, Kensington, London, W.
Todhunter, Dr. J., Orchardcroft, Bedford Park, London, W.
Toynbee Hall Library, Commercial St., Whitechapel, E. (*By grant.*)
Tozer, Rev. Henry Fanshawe, 10, Norham Gardens, Oxford.
Tregaskis, James, 4, Vernon Chambers, Southampton Row, London, W.C.
Trinity College, Library, Dublin
Turnley, E. J., Secretaries' Office, Inland Revenue, Somerset House, W C.
Tutin, J. R., Savile Street, Hull.
Tyrer, C. E., Manchester and Salford Bank, Manchester.
University College Library, Gower St., London, W.C. (*By grant.*)
Unwin, T. Fisher, 26, Paternoster Square, London, E.C.
Verrall, A. W., 3, Newnham Terrace, Cambridge.
Vezin, Hermann, 10, Lancaster Place, Strand, London, W.C.
Vian, Alfred, 17, Claverton Street, London, S.W.
Vian, Alsager, 3, Craven Street, Strand, London, W.C.
Waldron, Laurence A., 13, Raglan Road, Dublin.
Walford, Osborn, 42, St. Augustine's Road, Camden Square, London, N.W.
Walhouse, M. J., 9, Randolph Crescent, Maida Vale, London, W.
Walker, John, Lees House, Dewsbury.
Walker, W., 18, Yonge Park, Finsbury Park, London, N.
Waller, Alfred Rayney, Low Ousegate, York.
Warren, Miss K. M., 205, Euston Road, N.W.
Warren, Mrs. Gouveneur K., Newport, Rhode Island, New York, U.S.A.
Way, W. Irving, Topeka, Kansas, U.S.A.
Weir, P. Jenner, Cherbury, Beckenham, Kent.
Wellesley College, Wellesley, c/o H. Sotheran & Co., 136, Strand, W.C.
Wernham, Ernest J., Secretary's Office, General Post Office, London, E.C.
Whale, Geo., Denholm, Shrewsbury Lane, Shooter's Hill, Kent.
Wharton, Henry T., 39, St. George's Road, Kilburn, London, N.W.
Whistler, Joseph Swift, 19, Holyoke House, Cambridge, Mass., U.S.A.
White, A. Cromwell, 3, Harcourt Buildings, Temple, London, E.C.
White, W. Hale, Park Hill, Carshalton, Surrey.
Whitehead, Miss Francis H., 31, Fitzjohns Avenue, South Hampstead, N.W.
Whiteley, George, 40, Liverpool Street, London, W.C.
Wilkinson, T. R., Manchester and Salford Bank, Manchester.
Williams, W. R., The Ryleys, Alderley Edge, Manchester.
Wilmot, J. G., Junior Carlton Club, Pall Mall, London, S.W.
Wilson, H., Heathcote, Red Hill, Surrey.
Wilson, Mrs., 3, Portland Terrace, Regent's Park, London, N.W.
Wise, T. J., 127, Devonshire Road, Holloway, London, N.

Withers, Alfred, Kingsgate, Cricklewood, London, N.W.
Woodberry, G. E., Beverly, Mass., U.S.A.
Woods, Mrs. H. G., 28, Holywell, Oxford.
Woolnough, W. W., 12, Canterbury Road, East Brixton, London, S.W.
Worcester Free Library, Mass., U.S.A., c/o Messrs. Trübner & Co. 57, Ludgate Hill, London, E.C..
Yale College Library, Yale University, New Haven, Conn., U.S.A. (given by Professor T. R. Lounsbury).
Yeo, Gerald, University College, Oxford.

(402 Members.)

The Committee appeal to every Member to use his best efforts to increase the Society's numbers, which should reach 500 by the end of 1887. Personal canvassing of all likely well-wishers is what is needed.

www.ingramcontent.com/pod-product-compliance
Lightning Source LLC
Chambersburg PA
CBHW030249170426
43202CB00009B/677